248. 8
PSY

D0571567

ANGER

ISSUES OF EMOTIONAL LIVING
IN AN AGE OF STRESS
FOR CLERGY AND RELIGIOUS

ANGER

ISSUES OF EMOTIONAL LIVING
IN AN AGE OF STRESS
FOR CLERGY AND RELIGIOUS

THE TENTH
PSYCHOTHEOLOGICAL SYMPOSIUM

DAVID E. DOIRON

MARY ANN FAY

E.J. FRANASIAK

BERNARD J. BUSH

CRAIG F. EVANS

THOMAS J. TYRRELL

MARIE HOFER

G. MARTIN KELLER

BRENDAN P. RIORDAN

JOHN A. STRUZZO

MIRIAM D. UKERITIS

EDITED BY BRENDAN P. RIORDAN

ADMINISTRATIVE OFFICE
LIBRARY

AFFIRMATION BOOKS
WHITINSVILLE, MASSACHUSETTS

Affirmation Books is an important part of the ministry of the House of Affirmation, International Therapeutic Center for Clergy and Religious, founded by Sr. Anna Polcino, S.C.M.M., M.D. Income from the sale of Affirmation books and tapes is used to provide care for priests and religious suffering from emotional unrest.

The House of Affirmation provides a threefold program of service, education, and research. Among its services are five residential therapeutic communities and two counseling centers in the United States and one residential center in England. All centers provide nonresidential counseling. The House sponsors a leadership conference each year during the first week of February and a month-long Institute of Applied Psychotheology during July. More than forty clinical staff members conduct workshops and symposiums throughout the year.

For further information, write or call the administrative offices in Boston, Massachusetts:

The House of Affirmation
22 The Fenway
Boston, Massachusetts 02215
617/266-8792

To
present and former residents
of the House of Affirmation
with love and gratitude

Published with ecclesiastical permission

First Edition
©1985 by House of Affirmation, Inc.

All rights reserved, including the right of reproduction in whole or in part, in any form or by any means, electronic or mechanical, including photocopying, or by any information storage and retrieval systems, without permission in writing from the publisher. Inquiries should be addressed to Editor, Affirmation Books, 22 The Fenway, Boston, MA 02215

Library of Congress Cataloging in Publication Data

Psychotheological Symposium (10th : 1984 : Boston, Mass., etc.)
    Anger : issues of emotional living in an age of stress for clergy and religious.

    1. Anger—Religious aspects—Christianity—Congresses.
I. Doiron, David E.   II. Riordan, Brendan P.   III. Title.
BV4627.A5P78   1984   241'.3   84-29031
ISBN 0-89571-022-6

Printed by
Mercantile Printing Company, Worcester, Massachusetts
United States of America

CONTENTS

Foreword

Far too often anger is used as an emotional tool to manipulate a group or a person. The expression of anger should never prevent our examining the consequences of actions. Anger is only one aspect of reality, not a threat to it. We do not allow members of a group to use anger in order to play on the guilt of others: "Who takes the blame this time?"

When we try to ignore or escape the inevitable differences of opinion or of interest, we do so at the price of becoming submissive to others and of ignoring or escaping our own sense of individuality and dignity. Without the expression of anger it is impossible for community members to know one another, and to meet one another's important and realistic needs. In a community where such feelings are not expressed there exist unresolved and unhealthy dependency struggles, rather than a mutual acceptance of realistic and shared needs and abilities.

It is my experience that persons in ministry function effectively only if they are comfortable with their own anger and that of others. Men and women in ministry are to teach a proper model of the whole Christ: a Christ who was meek on some occasions and freely shared his anger at other times.

It is my hope that the reflections on anger in this book, edited by the Reverend Brendan P. Riordan, will challenge your thought and encourage your faith. Taken seriously, these essays could assist you in living life with a new sense of happiness.

Thomas A. Kane, Ph.D., D.P.S.
Priest, Diocese of Worcester
Publisher, Affirmation Books
Boston, Massachusetts
7 January 1985

Preface

In both religious circles and society in general, few words arouse greater interest than anger. But even today, while religious personnel are more willing than ever to acknowledge anger and even rage as important to the way we conduct our lives, maintain our relationships, relate with authority, and pray, there is still an urgent need for greater understanding of this powerful force. We need to develop the coping skills necessary for dealing with anger's many faces and consequences.

The tenth annual House of Affirmation symposium considered the subject of anger. The present volume, *Anger: Issues of Emotional Living in an Age of Stress for Clergy and Religious*, examines this issue from several points of view. As anger has its genesis in frustration, the essays presented here emphasize the frustration found in the lives of today's committed and struggling religious ministers: the frustration of living in community with angry and unhappy persons; the frustration of maintaining healthy, loving, and celibate relationships; the frustrating helplessness experienced in the midst of ecclesial, political, and global injustices; and the frustration and guilt of anger even toward God.

These essays will prove especially helpful to the persons who seek not only to admit to anger in their own lives, but who are also willing to "own" that anger and recognize it as a powerful and liberating source of energy for personal and historical change. The authors recognize anger as not only a "ferocious lion going about seeking to devour," but also an emotion that can be tamed to become a helpmate in our search for creativity.

I am grateful to the speakers who presented papers at our symposia in Boston, Middletown, San Francisco, St. Louis, and

Tampa. I also wish to thank the thousands of people who attended these sessions. Each audience added much to the presentations by its attentiveness, spontaneity, and provocative questions and insights, as well as expressions of appreciation. The evaluation forms received from those in attendance were a great source of affirmation to us. We also gladly accepted any comments that challenged us to continue to meet the needs of the ministers we seek to serve.

Many persons associated with the House of Affirmation have contributed to the success of this year's symposia. While I am prevented by limited space to name each person separately, I must especially thank the moderators who, through personal style, charisma, and much good humor, succeeded in setting the smooth and relaxed tone of each day: Rev. John Allan Loftus, S.J., Ph.D. (Boston), Rev. Joseph Hart, S.S.E., Ph.D. (Middletown), Rev. J. William Huber, Ph.D. (St. Louis), and Rev. Gerald Fath, O.P., D.Min. (Tampa). I consider myself privileged to be included among their number as the moderator of the San Francisco symposium.

We are also grateful to those who extended hospitality for the gatherings: the Sisters of St. Joseph at Aquinas Junior College in Newton; the Sisters of Mercy at Mercy High School in Middletown; the Sisters of the Presentation in San Francisco; the staff of St. John's Mercy Hospital in St. Louis, and the staff and congregation of the Church of Christ the King in Tampa.

At each House of Affirmation center sponsoring a symposium, former residents of our program are invited back on these occasions to maintain close friendships, share personal chapters in the stories of their life-journeys, and find renewed strength and encouragement. These reunions are great sources of joy and satisfaction to those of us who embrace this special healing ministry. It is for these women and men that we reserve our deepest personal gratitude.

Rev. Brendan P. Riordan
House of Affirmation
Boston, Massachusetts
5 December 1984

Anger and personal power

David E. Doiron

Rage near our center • Anger transformed • Five steps •
Self-determination • Responsibility • Re-union through love

*Reverend David E. Doiron, D. Min., is a psychotherapist at the House of
Affirmation in Hopedale, Massachusetts. He pursued his graduate education
at the University of Louvain, Belgium, and Assumption College, Worcester,
Massachusetts, and received a doctorate in ministry from Andover Newton
Theological Seminary. Before joining the staff of the House of Affirmation,
Father Doiron was director of the Wachusett satellite of the Worcester
Pastoral Counseling Center and chief psychological evaluator and tribunal
judge for the Diocese of Worcester Marriage Tribunal. Father Doiron is a
member of the American Association of Pastoral Counselors and the Ameri-
can Association of Marriage and Family Counselors.*

Anger and its expression have been problems throughout
human existence. In our culture there are many taboos against
expressing anger because we do not have models of how it can be
helpful and positive. Behind the taboos is oftentimes fear—fear of the
violence and destruction we have seen resulting from anger.

The process of acting out anger in verbal or physical abusiveness
short-circuits the anger-to-power process at its earliest stage, prevent-
ing people from touching their power and leaving them in a vicious
cycle of powerlessness. The cycle of harm and remorse makes people
weaker, more hopeless, and less effective.

Therefore the question is how to channel the incredible, potentially violent energy of anger; how to move forward; how to be fully
who we are within the constraints of the real world, and express
ourselves creatively without harm to anyone.

Love and forgiveness are essential to transforming anger, but
they are distortions when divorced from personal power—not necessarily power over others but power to act in concert with one's own
convictions. Whenever someone feels anger, there is a potential for
powerful dignity, a sense of responsibility, and the expression of some
deep personal value that has a universal rightness. This value needs
acknowledgement. Yet, because in moments of anger there is also a

potential for violence and aggression, this process is frequently suppressed.

Because anger is thought to be disrespectful and dangerous, parents and authority figures often disapprove of and suppress our expressions of anger. When this happens, the energy may find its way into other behaviors. This distorted expression can hurt others as with sarcasm, or ourselves with illnesses such as cancer, arthritis, or ulcers. Illness may develop after years of outwardly showing only our "nice" sides and inwardly feeling resentful and powerless.

When anger is channeled constructively it can result in personally powerful behavior. It can increase self-knowledge and appreciation, self-direction and self-expression.

Rage near our center

In a Jules Feiffer cartoon, Bernard says, "People are always saying the same thing about me. 'Bernard, you don't have a center,' they tell me. 'It's ok in your twenties not to have a center, but now you're forty-five. You've got to find your center.' Well, ten years ago I did find my center; it had sharp white teeth and ate people. Let those who can handle it have a center. I'll stick to my edges."

Our anger and rage, our "sharp white teeth," are indeed closely connected with our center. Rage is not the center itself, however, and at times what we call asserting ourselves is not assertion but aggression. Aggressive, impotent rage can evoke unpleasant responses which overwhelm us. I can angrily say within the boss's earshot, "She promised to help me and now changes her mind. We'll see if I do anything for her." I ventilate my rage and end up in a weak position. I show my sharp white teeth but without a sense of solid power.

Our impotent rage is not really our center. However, by deciding to stop its expression we do stop the expression of our center—our unique viewpoint which contains power, creativity, and vitality. When we are disconnected from our anger we are also alienated from our center, leaving us feeling depressed and powerless.

We can return to our center by going through the anger to its power source within us. It is like an immense force field. We discover that we are part of something bigger than ourselves. Our adversaries are also a part of it; we can exchange it. The anger actually leads us to our center which is connected to the center of the universe.

We must try to understand the origin of our anger. When we were infants we felt fully in control of our world. We expressed our needs and the world of big persons responded. Sooner or later there came a time when they resisted or ignored us. Anger was then the added force necessary to keep us noticed and taken care of. We needed to survive and continue to function, explore, and create new experiences within the limitations of the real world around us. Sometimes adults or siblings punished this healthy expression of rage. Then our rage became divorced from our sense of power and attached itself to guilt, insecurity, and hopelessness.

Anger transformed

Anger is a natural healthy experience of our power meeting resistance. We need to hold to the power and find the most satisfying and effective way to express it instead of being taken over by the experience of hopelessness. But we need to honor both the power in ourselves and the resistance in the other person.

When our anger enables us to contact our power we say that it has been transformed. It becomes an expression of self-assertion, of self-protection, of self-expression—a way of establishing our boundaries, creating our identity. If it does not get transformed, a number of things may happen. The energy can simply be dissipated, or it can be transformed in unhealthy ways. For instance, the anger may be reflected back upon us because of certain role expectations or beliefs such as "anger is not allowed in this convent," or "I'll be sent to Siberia." Many times this anger gets expressed as self-hatred, depression, psychosomatic illnesses, anxiety, or low self-esteem.

This can happen when the energy is transferred to a subpersonality often called "the critic." For example, we are angry, but our critic says, "Oh, Oh! Watch out. Good religious don't get angry. You must be charitable. To say something would not be Christian. Can't you forgive? There must be something wrong with you."

In this case our parent-critic has absorbed all the energy from the anger and is keeping the child in us imprisoned, always making us feel guilty and depressed. We may become compliant Sister Mary Perfecta, the mystical nun, so good, so pure, all light and grace, but not very human.

At times we may be aware of our anger but unable to express it. The anger becomes absorbed by "the king," another sub-personality with rigid expectations.

Five steps toward transforming anger

I would now like to give an example of anger transformed into personal power as developed by Walter Polt, and examine the five steps involved in this transformation.[1]

As I drive down the interstate one day, I approach a road construction area in which my lane of traffic is to merge right. I try to get ahead of the white pickup truck to my right rather than fall back and move into line behind it. The driver is unyielding, and I am forced to brake sharply and stop between the orange barrels in my disappearing lane.

I feel enraged. I yell at the white truck disappearing in the distance. My catharsis feels incomplete as I rail at the driver's stubbornness and call him names for his unconcern for my safety. I carry it further. I imagine pulling alongside him and shouting at him; I imagine shaking him. As my tears well, I recognize an old hurt and rage at having been heartlessly and coldly humiliated. My childhood floats into view, along with shades of competition and defeat. I have not only been forced aside, I have been humiliated. I have automatically taken step one in the anger-to-power process; I have established what is wrong.

I swing into step two, "I'd prefer." In my fantasy I tell the driver of the white truck what I would have preferred—not just to have been let into his lane of traffic, but for him to have yielded, to have shown forgiveness and concern for my feelings. I would have wished to feel a gentleness that protected my easily threatened self-image, my self-esteem.

With a further welling up of sadness and gratitude (an enriching sort of catharsis) I notice and embrace my spontaneous, ready concern for people's dignity and self-esteem. Step three, "This is me," has evolved naturally.

Because of the inner process I have experienced thus far, I see the possibility that the driver did not have the faintest idea of what he had done. I experience a deep satisfaction in myself and embrace my personal choice to support dignity in myself and other people. As an expression of step four, "You're ok where you are," I say to the driver mentally, "I respect you just as you are in your own life process."

In this case no direct expression of my anger to the "culprit" was ever necessary in order for my process to be complete. My step five, "Action plan," is simple: I immediately bring more respect, dignity, and courtesy into my driving as I re-enter the flow of traffic.

This example outlines a process and provides a framework and specific skills to move from anger to power. Let us review it.

Step one: What's wrong?

Step one answers the question, "What's wrong?" What do I feel like doing or saying to "let off steam"? The purpose of this step is to experience the raw anger, to get rid of the cork holding it in, to identify the hurt, threat, or wrong that triggered the anger. For example, "I feel really angry that you prevented me from merging into your lane of traffic. This action threatened my safety and my self-esteem." Or, "I feel really hurt, neglected, and angry that you tell me your gripes but don't make the time to listen to mine."

This step is generally done inwardly or separate from the person who has excited the anger. It is like starting a car that has been sitting unused. The initial smoke, the banging, coughing, and powerless roaring precede the experience of real power. When we consider these preliminaries bad or useless and shut the process down, we accumulate more smoke for later. We also shut down a larger process and make it more difficult to get to the powerful experience of a cleanly running engine. Others do not need our blue smoke in their faces, but they do need us to get to our power. When we are angry we do this part of the process separate from the culprits because the blue smoke may do harm to them and to our relationship with them.

In her book, *Anger, the Misunderstood Emotion*, Carol Tavris cites studies showing that the ventilationist approach does not reduce anger and stress but increases them.[2] Yet, I still support the ventilation of feelings—not for its own sake, but to reach the belief or value powering the anger.

While it is not always appropriate to vent anger directly at someone, there are ways to do it without making the other person a victim, but rather a loved and respected ally. George Bach and Peter Wyden in their book *The Intimate Enemy* suggest a useful kind of venting called "the fair fight."[3] The authors teach couples to establish rules for their venting. It is like putting on gloves, setting the boxing arena. If we establish boundaries and a safe context, we can say anything knowing that it is not meant to knock the other out, but to get to the bottom of some division.

By choosing ways to fight or making up rituals to express raw feelings we are saying, "I'm not destroying you or getting control; I'm getting to the bottom of my feelings." Just asking permission may be enough: "I need to tell you how angry I am. Do you have a safe place for listening to it now?" The partner can agree or say, "I'm putting the kids to bed. How about going for a walk in an hour?"

There may be many levels of "wrong" experienced, so this process may need to be used repeatedly with the same issue to unearth various kinds of insight and power. Take, for example, a childhood experience of deprivation, abuse, rape, or a tragedy of any kind. These incidents threaten us in various ways, and contain wrongs of many kinds. Step one, however, "What's wrong?" is the crucial stage. If we bypass the energy of the "steam" we will eventually need to come back to it. Sometimes we find it necessary to ventilate partially and move on, but if we go after all that is available right now, the subsequent stages will feel even more satisfactory.

While this first step is extremely important, it is essential that once the anger is out we not stop here. At this point we are very vulnerable to fear and guilt. If we end the process here, then we are left feeling unfinished, separate, and alone. The only recourse seems to be to express the anger over and over again. The result can be escalation of the angry feelings, vengeance, guilt, or self-punishment.

Step two: I'd prefer

The purpose of this step is to identify our positive preferences. "I would have preferred that you let me merge in front of you—that you had shown more concern for my safety and self-esteem and allowed for my mistake." Or, "I'd prefer that you stop taking so much time for your frustrations and start making more time for mine." In step two the word *prefer* is important. Whether or not someone else complies with our preference, our preference stands. We are taking responsibility for our own experience, not for someone else's behavior. The purpose of step two is to experience our personal positive preference, not to control someone else. If we go through step one and then experience in step two the shift to expressing our preference, we know a feeling of power. No authority in the world can stop us from holding our personal preferences.

Step three: This is me

The spotlight has now been taken off the "wrong" behavior of the other person and placed on ourselves and our own preferences. Step two is complete when we clearly know and experience our preferences in a specific situation. This leads naturally to step three in which we open our eyes to who we are as revealed by our preferences regarding the incident. For example, "I believe in allowing for mistakes, and respecting my own and others' safety and self-esteem." Or, "I really believe that my own gripes and the gripes of those close to me are worth listening to."

In step three we have arrived at the source of our power which was only hinted at by our anger or rage. That source is an important personal and human value that was apparently being threatened. It is a profound positive quality essential to our integrity and uniqueness. From step two, a statement of a specific preference related to someone else, we move to step three, a statement of a universal quality in ourselves. From "I prefer that you be on time" we move to "I choose to be punctual myself." At the moment of noticing that this quality is important to us, we are in contact with our depths.

Commitment, not consistency, is needed at this point. It is important to own the quality underlying the preference even when we notice parts of us that contradict it.

Even if we failed to live up to this principle yesterday, it is still true. It is a part of us now and always. Those other parts, those contradicting patterns of behavior, can make room for this one. They have their own positive qualities which will ultimately emerge as complementary, not contradictory, to this experience. This is what I think Walt Whitman means when he says in *Song of Myself*, "You say I am inconsistent? So, I am inconsistent. I am immense. I contain multitudes." If we have betrayed this principle in the past, it is even more important now to experience it fully, own it, and allow it appropriate expression. This strong commitment to ourselves is necessary, for without it the forgiveness and love of step four make no sense.

Step four: You're ok where you are

The purpose of step four is to experience the power in our preference while allowing ourselves to feel compassion and love for the culprit. For example, "I believe in respecting others' safety and self-esteem, and I let my love flow to you just as you are." Or, "I would strongly prefer that you listen more. Meanwhile, I'm letting my love flow to you just as you are."

Step four merges the power of our preference with the overflowing love at our center. The strength and love are important to each other.

Our personal standards and our forgiving love are complementary, not contradictory qualities. Ultimately, they are one. As we grow to understand and own our personal preferences, it becomes easier for us to be forgiving and loving of others. If this fourth step is impossible, we may need to own our preference and our power more profoundly and fully. We may need to notice our true capacity for love and clarify the kind of love involved here.

Like the power found in our anger, this love is greater than ourselves; it is compassion and an understanding of humankind. It recognizes each human being as struggling on a unique path—a path beyond the comprehension of our smaller selves. There is a part of us and every human being that sees each individual with objectivity and compassion. It is this part that we draw on when we allow our love to flow to those for whom we feel anger and whose behavior we would like to see changed. This part of ourselves is capable of love and forgiveness even before the other person has "shaped up" according to our preferences.

This loves comes not so much out of superhuman effort but out of a letting go—a releasing of demands, of expectations, or of conditions that we place on our love. An easily understood example of this kind of love and forgiveness is seen in the mother who is angry with her child for slamming the door behind him every time he goes out of the house. She continues to love the child even though this behavior has not yet changed.

It may not be so easy to love this way in the case of anger at a person who has harmed us or a friend, but the principle is the same. We are not fully mature human beings unless we know what our preferences are. Nor are we fully mature unless we allow our love to flow to everyone, even though they do not live up to our preferences.

It is even possible at times to experience the power in step three so deeply that we feel that we are at the center of our being. Then step four has already happened. Our power has a gentleness that is tantamount to love. Eastern thought says that true joy rests on firmness and strength within, manifesting itself outwardly as yielding and gentle.

When we say, "I hold this position *and* I love you where you are," we are expressing a forgiveness that comes out of strength, not weakness. True forgiveness does not include giving up our dignity or integrity or cooperating with someone else's hurtful patterns of behavior. If we cooperate with those patterns we may further debilitate the other person as well as allow harm to ourselves.

In a Blondie cartoon, Dagwood says to Blondie, "Honey, could you love me under any conditions?" She says, "Of course." He says, "What if I quit my job, squandered all our money, and became a complete bum? Would you love me then?" "Yes," she says, "and I'd write to you from wherever I was." Blondie is saying that in the situation presented by Dagwood, her love would continue, but she would protect herself by separating from him.

The process so far has been focused on experiencing our power rather than doing something with it. What is important now is to carry the inner experience of our power into action, using it in the outside world.

Step five: Action plan

Once we have restarted a neglected car, blown off the blue smoke, and experienced power again, we have many choices as to where to drive the car. We have the opportunity now to choose where to direct our power; what action do we want to take? We may say, for example, "Before driving I pause to relax and to experience compassion and tolerance. Other drivers are as fallible as I am." Or, "I will keep on loving you, and I will arrange for equal time for both of us."

We have many alternatives for stopping or checking violent or unjust behavior. In some cases we may choose to listen, and in others we may wish to communicate our feelings. How we express our feelings is important. Getting to our own value first is more beneficial than venting as we go along. Just "dumping" our feelings does not always work well; people often react defensively.

It is important, however, for us to express our feelings once we have examined them. For example, we may need to change things now—get someone off our toe. Or we may need to find out why things should not change. It is also important at times to be heard, even if we are merely planting seeds for future changes. If we leave our message unspoken, withhold our unique seed-thoughts, they may never germinate and grow. Sometimes we should express our feelings simply to be understood as a person.

An alternative plan may be to give the key phrases backwards, beginning with, "I believe in being punctual, and I do still love you." Now steps two and one have an effect: "I would have preferred that you got here on time. You're late, and I feel really angry."

Self-determination

The process of transformation, of moving from anger to power, involves moving to deeper and deeper levels. The first level is getting at the anger and letting it come out. Sometimes the emotion goes beyond anger to hatred, hostility, and even what I call murderous rage. This is especially true if there has been much denial of anger over a long period of time.

One can almost measure the depth of murderous rage by the level of self-denial present. Letting this rage out helps differentiate us. It separates us from what or whom we are merged with—priest or religious made one with mother or father, husband and wife fused together, undifferentiated in an infantile and unhealthy way. By yelling or getting out the anger, we carve out our person, separate from others. The child who for the first time blasts out a "no" to his mother is expressing his awareness of himself as separate and distinct from her.

However, there is danger in stopping at the level of anger, hatred, or murderous rage—the danger that the anger will be reflected back to us in the form of self-hatred. We have to move to deeper levels of feeling under the anger, to connect with the pain, sadness, despair— and under that, love—so we can touch other aspects of the relationship and make a connection.

Responsibility

We are then in the process of getting in touch with our power which comes from the energy released through anger. This power emerges from self-expression and self-knowledge, and needs to be linked with responsibility—responsibility for who we are, as well as for the parts of us that get us into situations of anger. Responsibility is an agent of transformation as well as an energetic flow. Once we take responsibility, we do not have to be angry in the same way. The anger is transformed into a positive quality of personal power: "I am here; I am responsible; I am free to choose what kind of relationships I will have with the Church, my husband, superior, friend, or parent."

Re-union through love

However, this power and self-determination untempered by wisdom, love, and patience, have the potential to corrupt or polarize. We may feel separated from others—unique, responsible, self-respecting, and deserving of love. Feeling our power and strength, the temptation to pride and selfishness is tremendous if we stay at this level. The final step in the process of anger-to-power involves uniting or blending with a quality of love, wisdom, or compassion. These virtues are needed so that our expression of power in relationship to Church, God, parent, or husband is tempered, and the experience of union which has always existed from a spiritual perspective is re-established or re-experienced.

In other words, the first attempt at union ended in fusion, with ourselves and our identity being wiped out. The expression of anger separated us and got us in touch with power—a sense of self, our own ego strength. From there we may proceed to re-union, true union, with parent, God, Church, ex-husband. This process allows us and the object of our anger to see ourselves as part of something larger.

Conclusion

There is a unity of love—a unity often blocked by the denial of anger. The way back to love and unity is through our anger. Many times we have a false image of spiritual life. Priests and religious often have a premature spiritual identity in which they feel they have to deny their anger when in reality they are mad as hell. This situation is also common in what is referred to as the New Age—people meditating for months in full lotus positions while they hate their fathers and live in fear of expressing it.

The questions we need to ask are what is the nature of the spiritual life and what is the nature of the spiritual community? How is spiritual life in community blocked by the denial of anger? It is obviously very difficult and painful for those of us who have chosen the sisterhood, brotherhood, or priesthood to be furious at everybody. It is painful and we feel guilty, so we go around trying to be nice. But at some level, all the time, we are yearning for something more. We are dying in the very places, the houses and centers where we should be finding that spiritual vision.

Piero Ferrucci in *What We May Be* says: "On this planet one person kills another every twenty seconds. One dollar out of six is given to military expenses. It costs $14,800 per year to maintain a soldier, versus $230 to educate a child. A gun is sold in the United States every 13 seconds. The tragically clumsy way in which humanity handles its own aggression generates massive destructiveness. We all realize that the solutions to this immense problem are difficult and extremely complex. But these shocking statistics suggest the importance of personal transformation as one of the many ways to deal with this critical situation. Sometimes we can succeed in turning our aggressive energy from destructive into constructive action."[4]

Finding new models for expressing anger is an exciting challenge for our time. It is an important quest for all of us.

Endnotes

1. The steps in the anger to power process were developed by Walter J. Polt in an unpublished article entitled "From Anger to Power."

2. Carol Tavris, *Anger: The Misunderstood Emotion* (New York: Simon and Schuster, 1982).

3. George Bach and Peter Wyden, *The Intimate Enemy* (New York: William Morrow, 1968).

4. Piero Ferrucci, *What We May Be* (Los Angeles, Cal.: J.P. Tarcher, 1982), p. 93.

Anger: Myths and meanings

Mary Ann Fay

Anger and aggression • Phases of anger •
The need to take charge • Misunderstandings •
The closed emotional circuit • The uses of anger •
Old myths • New myths • A challenge to grow

Mary Ann Fay, Ph.D., a full-time psychotherapist at the House of Affirmation in Whitinsville, Massachusetts, is a licensed psychologist and a member of the graduate faculty at Emmanuel College in Boston. She received her doctoral degree from Boston University, and served as coordinator of the Readiness for Ministry program at Boston University School of Theology. Dr. Fay is a psychological consultant to the United Methodist Church, and has offered workshops on the psychology of religion, assertiveness, personality development, and women's studies. She is a member of the American Psychological Association, divisions of the psychology of women, and psychologists interested in religious issues, and a member of the Society for the Scientific Study of Religion.

When I began to write this essay on anger I realized that I faced the task with trepidation. It struck me that anger has a unique capacity to evoke a chain of powerful reactions in us, not the least of which is fear. Small wonder, then, that we are unnerved by its appearance.

Anger is a basic event in the lives of all of us, yet philosophers and social scientists cannot seem to agree on a definition. Like fire, it is easier to recognize than to analyze or extinguish. Often, it generates more heat than light. However, I will attempt to illuminate some aspects of the origins and meanings of anger from different perspectives.

The social psychologist Carol Tavris relates this interesting tale from India. A cobra who dwelt by the side of a road leading to the temple began to attack and bite people on their way to worship. The Swami, hearing of the people's fear, explained to the creature the error of its ways. He was able to obtain from the cobra a promise to stop its troublesome behavior. As time went on, however, the townspeople grew unafraid of the snake. Some local boys went so far as to drag the snake around in play. The cobra, battered and bleeding, appealed to the Swami for help. The Swami, gazing in consternation at the abused creature, exclaimed, "I told you not to bite, but I did not tell you not to hiss."[1]

Anger and aggression

Who of us has not confused biting with hissing? We have difficulty differentiating between aggression and anger, perhaps because the distinction between them can be very slight. Does raising one's voice to express the emotion of anger constitute aggression? Or is aggression only present if the raised voice carries explicit rather than implicit threat?

Also at issue is whether aggression is intrinsic or extrinsic to human nature. Even within psychoanalysis, perhaps the most powerful psychological movement of the twentieth century, there is debate on the topic. Freud felt that libido, the life instinct, and the instinct of aggression were the two primary drives of the human person. Much of life, he believed, was structured around the individual's attempt to keep these powerful unconscious forces in precarious balance.

Other thinkers in the psychoanalytic tradition took issue with this theory, however. They believed that infants are not born with an aggressive instinct, but rather develop it as a consequence of too much frustration of their need for dependent parental relationships. Parents are charged with the challenging task of allowing enough frustration for their child to learn appropriate self-reliance, but not enough to engender the rage of true deprivation. However, as products of their own families, they rarely succeed in providing optimal care for their infants. The cycle of frustration-evoked aggression thus continues.

There are many other hypotheses regarding the basis of anger and aggression. While we cannot be certain of the origins of anger and aggression, we can examine their occurrence in our own lives.

We know from experience that anger is a feeling of hostile displeasure that follows our perception that we have been injured in some way. No matter what its origin, we may agree that anger is a common event in our daily lives. Nevertheless, some of us get angry more often than others, and an event that angers one person leaves another unaffected. If we are particularly sophisticated, we may selectively protect ourselves from being provoked by others. As an acquaintance of mine once said, "You can't get my goat if you don't know where it's tied."

Phases of anger

We can explain our differing experiences of anger in several ways. However, I would like to consider from a cognitive perspective the four different stages in the unfolding of the interpersonal anger response.[2]

The cognitive phase begins with an awareness of another's behavior and proceeds to an interpretation of that behavior. If we believe the behavior is directed toward us, and does us undeserved injury, the stage is set for phase two.

In the physiological phase we begin to have specific bodily changes; the muscles tighten and changes in respiration and circulation take place. There may be obvious signs such as clenched fists or a reddened face.

In the third, emotional phase of the anger response, the angry person experiences pain or displeasure at the injury and enmity or dislike for the provocator.

Finally, in the fourth or conative phase, the urge to retaliate arises. This may or may not be expressed in overt, hostile behavior toward the provocator.

While this cycle is quite complex, an individual experiencing it may have different degrees of awareness. Also, how quickly the process moves can vary considerably; we may burn slowly or have a short-fuse explosion.

The key to understanding our angry responses can be found in the first, cognitive phase of development. We have to perceive that another's objectionable behavior is somehow directed toward us, or toward someone with whom we are closely identified. That is, we have to personalize the other's behavior. We vary a great deal in our tendency to do this. Some people become enraged at Boston drivers running red lights while others wait and wax philosophical about the computer systems that regulate traffic signals.

The development of anger depends on the belief that the injury we experience is intentional. Occasionally, failing to find intentional behavior, we assign responsibility for behavior. If a tree in my neighbor's yard falls on my car during a storm, I will not blame my neighbor. I might, however, grow angry with him for not noticing that the tree was diseased and ready to fall. Perhaps the weather forecaster or God could share the blame as well.

Finally, to grow angry we must believe that the injury we experience is unjustified. However, the human capacity to deny the justice of punishing experiences is remarkable. We are experts at finding extenuating circumstances for our actions. Indeed, when psychologists discover a person who freely acknowledges being deserving of insult or injury, that person is suspected of masochism!

The need to take charge

There is considerable choice involved in the experience of becoming angry. We are used to assuming responsibility for our behavior, but less accustomed to claiming responsibility for our feelings. The latter dynamic reduces our power, leaving us with a sense of relative helplessness.

Obviously, the more aware we are of our inner states, and the more able we are to monitor subtle cues in our own behaviors, the more choice and power we have. A common fear is that our anger is irrational. However, from a cognitive perspective, anger is both a rational and an affective experience. If anything is irrational, it is the way we interpret the behavior of others, or the "oughts and shoulds" we have for them. In *Gulliver's Travels* the Lilliputians went to war with the Brobdingnagians over which end of the egg to open!

Misunderstandings

Sometimes psychologists and other mental health professionals say of an individual, "He has a reservoir of anger," or, "She's been burying resentment for years." This is expressive language, but it is important to understand it as metaphor, rather than as psychological geography. We are not hollow pits full of feelings, but complex individuals with particular styles of experiencing and processing emotion.

Some of us have made value judgments about certain feelings. Many religious people have misunderstood the Golden Rule as a command to short-circuit so-called negative emotions like anger or jealousy. However, there is a subtle but powerful reality in our emotional lives: continually thwarting one group of emotions has a stunting effect on all the rest. Constantly blocking anger has a disabling effect on the entire personality. As a result, a person who seems to have a "reservoir of anger" might be suffering from great sadness, loneliness, or pain, and might lack the skill to express these emotions.

The closed emotional circuit

At times we develop what might be called a closed emotional circuit. A few years ago I complained to a friend that my alma mater continually misspelled my name on the mail it sent. After listening to my grousing, my friend said to me, "Well, if it bothers you so much, why don't you just call them and ask them to change the spelling?" To which I relied, "Oh, no, I'm much too angry about it to talk to them!"

Of course, we all know how foolish such behavior can be. However, I think such emotional closed-circuits are more common than we care to admit. They operate not only within individuals, but within groups. Families and other intentional communities that live intimately with one other are prone to what might be called closed-circuit scripts. In such a script, each party is locked into a particular response-set that is automatic, unexamined, and circular. Anger is often central in these scripts. A family therapist tells the story of a thirty-year-old woman who had sought counseling because she felt dominated by her mother.

The daughter recounted that whenever she walked in the door of her parents' home for a visit, her mother began to order her about. "Did you hang up your coat in the closet? Hang it up. What did you have for breakfast? What do you mean, you didn't have breakfast?" After several hours the daughter's patience would wear thin and she would begin to complain, "Mother, you treat me like a child."

"Well, what do you expect when you don't even know enough to eat your breakfast?" her mother would respond. This exchange would be followed by the daughter's loss of patience. Shouting and stamping her foot, she would cry, "I'm not a two-year-old, mother. I'm not, I'm not!"

Changing such an emotional closed-circuit implies examining the behavior and understanding the function of the emotions being expressed. Although many individuals fear that expressing anger will destroy their close relationships, anger is sometimes used as the psychic glue to hold a relationship together. Martha and George in *Who's Afraid of Virginia Woolf* used anger as the coin of exchange in their relationship.

In families where individual boundaries are so poorly drawn that members think and speak for each other, anger is often the major emotion expressed. It serves to relieve the suffocating pseudocloseness which is really a lack of differentiation among family members.

It is also a way of expressing emotion without risking the threatening vulnerability of statements of warmth, caring, or dependence. The anger demonstrated in this situation is apt to be of the closed-circuit variety, rather than a more considered, less rigid mode of response. Though the family is the prototype of this closed system, other groups that live in close, emotional bonding may fall into such patterns of behavior.

The uses of anger

We can use anger in either a productive or a nonproductive manner. We can utilize anger to let another person know when our boundaries have been transgressed. Like the hiss of the cobra, anger can be a powerful warning sign that we are not to be treated badly. The Christian message of turning the other cheek, of freely going the second mile when we are forced to go the first, is a message of moral choice. Choice, of course, implies freedom to choose. I suspect that the meek who shall inherit the earth will be very powerful people.

One of the most helpful ways to evaluate anger is to consider it as communication. If we are frightened or anxious in relationship, we can utilize anger as a protective shield. We have all had the experience of being in the company of a person for whom anger is almost an aura. There is a diffuse and undifferentiated quality to such a person's anger. The message it communicates, however, is clear: keep your distance. We can only speculate upon the message behind the distancing behavior. However, the feeling of being threatened commonly underlies this dynamic.

On the other hand, we can use our anger to communicate our desire to be close to someone. Such anger is apt to be direct and coherent, an event rather than an attitude. Unlike the more diffuse, distancing anger, it gives way without extreme difficulty to the full range of other emotions. We are less apt to get "stuck" in the kind of anger that supports trust and honesty.

Old myths

This brings us to some of the old and new myths regarding anger. An old myth states that anger is an emotion to be suppressed on most occasions. Many children have been taught by virtue of swift punishment that any display of temper is unacceptable. The message that anger is bad was a powerful one.

The only exception made to this precept was what might be called "righteous anger." We all have echoing in our memories sermons or religion classes about the just anger of Jesus as he drove the money changers out of the temple. The only problem with this exception is that the vast majority of our angry moments are elicited by what we perceive as personal injury. We do not usually defend the rights or the honor of others to the point of anger. Furthermore, it is questionable as to whether children have the developmental capacity to experience such righteous anger. In any event, suppressing anger was naively thought to build strength of character. Resentment was actually a more likely outcome.

New myths

A new myth about anger concentrates on evaluating the expression rather than the essence of anger. According to the new myth, which pop psychology supports, suppressing anger is unhealthy or neurotic behavior. Concomitantly, expressing anger leads to health, satisfaction, and personal calm. Actually, there is evidence to suggest that constant expressions of anger lead to yet more anger. Given enough emphasis, most human behaviors can become self-reinforcing.

Demonstrating anger indiscriminately can be naive, foolish, or downright dangerous. Emotions have power that requires monitoring. In the case of anger, issues of strength and weakness are primary. For example, children are often victimized by the anger of the very adults who forbid them the expression of their own.

The demonstration of emotion is not automatically health-producing in itself. What is true is that we need access to our anger and we need a network of relationships in which anger can be safely expressed. This is another way of saying that in our relationships it is good to be free to communicate by means of anger when that is what we truly feel. While suppression of anger in many life circumstances might be wise, habitual suppression of anger in personal relationships breeds apathy and alienation.

Another myth is that anger must be rigidly controlled or it will break social bonds within a relational system, such as a family or community. Various cultures have taboos against the demonstration of anger in certain social situations, but provide approved outlets for aggression. The football games following the familial celebrations of

Thanksgiving and New Year's Day may provide such an avenue for aggressive impulses. Be that as it may, the reality is that most of the social systems we create with family, friends, and colleagues are basically stable enough to absorb the expression of anger.

Anger: A challenge to grow

However, it is also true that expressing anger within even a well-established social system may breed anxiety and upset the balance of power. This occurrence is not necessarily bad; it may even be creative. Since systems are geared to seek and maintain homeostasis, the expression of anger is a test of a system's flexibility and power to adapt. Open emotional expression can be an agent of growth. Furthermore, systems are generally able to deal with anger that is too disruptive by powerful internal controls. While we may have a deep fear that expressing anger makes things fall apart, this idea is often more fantasy than reality.

Anger is a potent reality that, like the hiss of the cobra, can affect our basic life experiences. Whether anger has its source in nature or nurture or both, it is clearly a universal experience. Social scientists know we can learn new emotional responses and we can learn to direct them to serve us. As long as we live, growing to understand our emotions and to adjust our attitudes about them is possible. Anger, which can both threaten and challenge us, can also be an enriching resource. Appreciating our anger is something like valuing the bubbling life within us.

Endnotes

1. D. Boyd, *Rolling Thunder* (New York: Random House, 1974) quoted in C. Tavris, *Anger: the Misunderstood Emotion* (New York: Simon and Schuster, 1982).
2. D. Kaplan and D.W. Goodrich, "A Formulation for Interpersonal Anger" (National Institute for Mental Health, 1950).

Betrayed: The anger of growing up

E. J. Franasiak

Trust in outer providers • Loss of innocence •
From dependency to consciousness

E. J. Franasiak, Ph.D., is director of the House of Affirmation in Hopedale, Massachusetts. He received his master's degree in psychology from Boston College, and his doctoral degree in clinical psychology from the Psychological Studies Institute, Palo Alto, California. Dr. Franasiak has been with the House of Affirmation since the first consulting center opened in Worcester, Massachusetts. He has served as a psychotherapist at the Whitinsville, Massachusetts center, and assistant director at Montara, California. He holds membership in the American Psychological Association and the American Academy of Psychotherapists.

There has always been a kind of popular and practical "vestibule" psychology found in small pamphlets at the back of churches. Among other troublesome human experiences, anger has been a favorite subject of these short "how to" treatises. One point consistently presented regarding anger is its sinfulness. This essential wisdom reflects Paul's letter to the Ephesians (4:26, 27): "Even if you are angry, you must not sin: never let the sun set on your anger or else you will give the devil a foothold."

This essay relies on the essential wisdom that anger can be sinful—that is, a denial rather than an affirmation of human life and the life of grace. It describes the powerful angry styles of revenge, denial, cynicism, inauthenticity, and perfectionism that can follow experiences of painful hurt, bitter disappointment, or severe loss. Finally, it considers the relationship between these angry responses and broken trust and its ultimate experience, betrayal.

Betrayal is always painful. It is also an unavoidable and essential experience of growing up by which the child can be transformed into the adult. Betrayal requires forgiveness. Out of the act of forgiveness, new consciousness, new growth, new life can emerge.

It is important to note at the outset that feelings of anger are not sinful. Behavior that appropriately expresses anger is not sinful. When we are very angry we need to experience and spontaneously express these thoughts and feelings in an appropriate manner. However, when anger or some form of it becomes a consistent life style, denying rather than affirming life, then anger has become sinful.

Trust in outer providers

Let us begin with a story. Once upon a time there were a father and a son. The building in which they lived was old and in disrepair. One evening after they went to bed a great fire broke out. The father ran out of the building thinking his son was safe, only to find that the son had climbed to the roof and was trapped. "Jump!" he called to his son. "I can't I can't," cried the child. "Jump!" begged the father. "I'm afraid, I can't," was the answer. The smoke thickened; the flames billowed. Again the father screamed, "Jump, son, jump. I'll catch you!" "No," screamed the child. "I'm afraid; I cannot see you." "*But I can see you*," cried the father. "Jump, now!" And the son jumped. The father caught him; the child was saved.

The key element in this story is trust. It is a story of basic trust between an innocent child in danger and a strong loving parent. It is a story that we can identify with from the point of view of the terrified child as well as the strong rescuing parent. This is a Christian love story: God's love for his people; the father's love for his daughter; the mother's love for her son. It is a parental love story; it touches the terrified child in each of us and calls up feelings of warmth, trust, safety, innocence. As father and son are united in each other's arms, our anxiety over the peril is relieved. We rejoice.

Trust in another is the first major hurdle of human development. It is basic to all relationships, major life events, and all of human development. Erikson wrote that trust is that original optimism, the assumption that somebody is there, without which we cannot live. When children do not learn trust because parents are inadequate or deficient, consequences are severe. "They do not respond, nor learn; they do not assimilate their food and even fail to defend themselves against infection and often die physically as well as mentally."[1]

The primary connection of the child to the parental figure in trust is critical. It reflects a primitive, instinctual response to a reliable and consistently available source. Trust in the parent is the beginning of trust in oneself. It is the foundation for every human relationship that follows. "The general state of trust . . . implies that one has learned to rely on the sameness and continuity of the outer providers."[2]

Children are radically dependent for their physical and emotional needs. Their dependence must be recognized, respected, and satisfied. Parents need to be available and dependable. They must neither betray nor exploit their child's vulnerability. The relationship of child to adult is not a peer relationship nor a relationship of equality; there is no mutual responsibility. It is a relationship where the mother is responsible for the daughter, and the daughter is responsible to or accountable to and dependent on the mother.

Contrary to what we often attribute to this relationship, an infant does not love its mother. It is not capable of loving. An infant makes a *needs response* to a parent or parental figure. An infant is in a totally subservient position and must not only submit to the wishes of the adult, but totally rely on the benign intention of the adult. The adult is in charge and in total control. Although we often speak of the child's love for the parent, it is closer to the truth that the child/parent relationship is a power relationship.

Only later, when mutuality is possible, is love possible. For many of us, trust in the wise parent has been a cornerstone of emotional and spiritual development. Implicit in this approach is the notion that if I trust completely—that is, jump even though I cannot see—I will be all right. I will be caught, saved, or made holy.

Those of us who have been fortunate enough to be trained in seminaries or novitiates or by Roman Catholic men and women religious in the last fifty years, have received a superior classical education. We have been taught to think critically and reason logically. We have been taught that it is not only logical, but correct that we submit to someone or something that is bigger, stronger, more knowledgeable, more powerful than we are. The reasons for such submission have been compelling.

Childlike trust, we were taught, would enable us to grow into the image and likeness of God and to attain salvation. If this long-term goal were not enough, there was the additional expectation that in the short-run we would be serene, happy, comfortable, and objectively right.

Now this approach of dependency and trust has its merits. We trust because we are weak, vulnerable, dependent, and helpless. Because of our condition, we have a relationship based on our need of another, a parental figure (or rule or law or condition) more powerful, more knowledgeable, and stronger than we are. We rely on the sameness and continuity of the outer provider, much as the child relies on its mother or father. Trust in someone or something bigger is useful, especially when we are clearly smaller.

This approach is particularly useful for adults who require a lot of structure, supervision, or clear lines of authority, or who work best in submission to certain corporate or group goals. Clearly that is some part of us all at times.

This paradigm of trust and dependency is not only practical; it is comfortable for both the child and the adult. From the point of view of the adult it implies that as long as you do what I say you will be all right. So will I. As long as you do not question my authority, I have no need to reflect on it. We stay in role. I maintain the position of the benevolent parent; you maintain the position of the obedient child. This is a practical and useful way to maintain things as they are. You do not make me angry and you do not feel my anger. I am superior and you need me to be superior. There is contentment in this imbalance, and commitment to maintaining the stasis.

Loss of innocence

I have another story. Again, it is about a father and son. This time the father is teaching his son how to trust by having the son jump off steps. The son climbs to the first step. The father says, "Jump." The son jumps and the father catches him. The son climbs to the second step. Again, the father urges him to jump. The son jumps and the father catches him. It happens a third, fourth, and fifth time. Each time the father urges the boy to jump. Each time the child takes the risk and each time he is caught. For the tenth time, the process is repeated. The boy climbs to the highest step, he jumps, the father steps back, and the son hits the floor! When he comes to, he is bruised and bloodied. The father says to him, "That will teach you not to trust authority even when it is your own father."

Story number two stands in marked contrast to story number one. Story number two leaves us with a strong sense of disbelief, anger, and helplessness. In a sense the story is itself a kind of betrayal of our expectation, a kind of derailment. It leaves us angry, with a sense of danger, injustice, unfairness, and outrage. How could this happen? How could this happen especially when everything was going so well?

Now this second story raises an interesting question. Do people need to learn not to trust?

To begin to answer this question, we turn to Mark's Gospel: When evening came he arrived with the Twelve. And while they were at table eating, Jesus said, "I tell you solemnly, one of you is about to betray me, one of you eating with me." They were distressed and asked him, one after another, "Not I, surely?" Peter said, "Even if all lose faith, I will not." Then Jesus said to him, "I tell you solemnly, this day, this very night before the cock crows twice, you will have disowned me three times" (Mark 14:18-30).

Peter said to him, "Why can't I follow you now? I will lay down my life for you." "Lay down your life for me?" answered Jesus. "I tell you most solemnly, before the cock crows you will have disowned me three times" (John 12:27-38).

We get the feeling that something very serious is going on: best friends coming to a falling out; trust in an intimate relationship about to be broken. It is not a petty issue here—not just hurting someone or being impolite, or insulting. There is something foreboding, laden with sin. Whatever is going to happen is going to cause some permanent changes.

"You will lay down your life for me, will you?" There is a note of sarcasm, disbelief, doubt—as if Jesus had already withdrawn from that support. Something inevitable is about to happen, not out of control, just inevitable. Something is about to be lost, never again to be recaptured.

What is betrayal? Betrayal is an experience of a loss of faith and hope in another person or institution. It is a disappointment of severe magnitude touching the depth of our being. It is loss of that which was dependable, consistent, and there for us.

Betrayal can be quick and devastating like the death of someone. More frequently it is subtle, an erosion of trust or confidence in a painfully tedious manner. Betrayal is often the insight culminating a history of painful human experience and leaving a person crushed, depleted, at a point of crisis—uncertain about going forward, but certain of not going back.

From dependency to consciousness

Recently I came across the following reflection: "My religious life has been completely taken over by professionals. If I want to learn to pray I go to a Spiritual Director; to discover God's will for me I go to a Retreat Master; to understand my Bible I go to a Scripture Scholar; to find out if I have sinned I go to the Moral Theologian; and to have my sins forgiven I go to the Priest."[3]

A critical aspect of trust is the sameness and continuity of the outer providers; a key aspect of betrayal is a break in the sameness and continuity of the outer providers. The provider is not just unreliable; the relationship does not work anymore!

When this break occurs—that is, when the outer provider changes or withdraws, our first response is to get terribly angry or afraid or depressed. We feel anger because we have been let down. We are afraid because we are thrown back on ourselves. We are depressed because our ego has been deflated, someone has "taken the steam" out of us. To be betrayed by the other is to be left standing alone.

Betrayal is the radical shift from dependency on the outer which is bigger, to the inner which is meager. Betrayal is trust in the other and outer being smashed and broken. Betrayal is a radical shift in dependency from the greater to the lesser, from the stronger to the weaker, from the mighty to the powerless, from clarity and authority to confusion and floundering. It challenges all my psychic achievements to date and thrashes my confidence in that which is greater and better. Betrayal utters from its depths, "My God, my God, why have you deserted me?" Betrayal is the fearful and reluctant beginning of autonomy.

Erikson explains that autonomy in its early stage is experienced as separateness from the parental figure. In adulthood, autonomy enables us to make decisions; we are empowered. Resolution of the betrayal, forgiveness, can result in empowerment.[4]

However, the immediate effects of betrayal are closer to shock. A betrayed person is numb and immobile. When the anger, hurt, and rejection are unresolved for a prolonged period, there is danger of becoming "the betrayed one," crucified by the other and permanently attached only to the cross. There are many ways this enmeshment with the cross, a suffering that is neither redemptive nor purgative, occurs. I mention only revenge, denial, cynicism, inauthenticity, and perfectionism.[5]

For some, revenge becomes the response: an eye for an eye and a tooth for a tooth. It trades mistrust for mistrust and suffering for suffering. There is no progress with revenge, no affirmation. Obsessive preoccupation with the other entails feuding, plotting, and fantasies of cruelty and vindictiveness.

For others, denial, the opposite of affirmation, is the response to betrayal: you were never the beloved. In anger and hatred and hurt we deny the value of the other person, the institution, the organization, or the effort. Where there has been blindness to the inherent weakness of the beloved, we now see only the ugliness, frailty, and humanity.

Another response is cynicism. The essence of virtue becomes self-control, non-involvement. To the abused wife, all men are bastards. To the disillusioned religious, the entire church is phony. To the priest who chooses to leave priesthood, all ministry is self-serving. To the rejected lover, all love is false.

The cynical person strikes out alone, angry, distrustful, and denying the other. The original idealism is broken and replaced with the new cynicism: "Reject before you are rejected," and, "Don't get involved with them."

As a relationship develops we open up in trust. Something of ourselves that we have held closely and have given to no one is shared: this is our secret, our authentic self. We are many things to many people, but this, this part of us is really our true self. We share it lovingly. Then in the rage of betrayal, this authentic self is in danger of being degraded or discarded.

This behavior is protective; we do not want to be hurt again—not again. We will never allow ourselves to open up, become vulnerable, or trust so completely or deeply again. "She wasn't worth it; he's a bastard; the Church is screwed up."

The last response, perfectionism, is yet another way of protecting ourselves. We will never again be betrayed if we build the perfect relationship, perfect community, perfect family, or perfect society.

The demand for loyalty, not openness, becomes all important. Any threat to security or suggestion of change cannot be tolerated. "You must never let me down" is the motto. Undying devotion and everlasting fidelity (never quite believed) become the themes of the relationship. That which is human is excluded. Continual reassurances of trust attempt to exclude the possibility of betrayal.

Conclusion

Love is based on trust, yet trust contains within it a seed of betrayal. Without the possibility of betrayal, the relationship is not really based on trust, but on power. Power enforces by rules or fear or inferiority. Love holds; love emerges out of the mutual power of two.

To live or love only when we can trust, when we are secure, contained, caught, when we cannot be hurt or disappointed, is to be outside of real life. Betrayal is a reality of human life. Whomever or whatever we trust—our friend, the Church, the community, the diocese, psychotherapy, law, relationships—we risk betrayal.

Often we are content to value fidelity at the expense of life, loyalty at the expense of truth. We confuse ignorance with innocence, and sacrifice maturity. We value unquestioned commitment to the old ways at the expense of creative and responsible decisions about present realities. We cling to a sterile but secure impotency, fearful that one tiny but powerful step may trip us up.

Betrayal is a painful and absolutely necessary human experience. It lies at the core of trust and love and adulthood. It is our initiation into fuller consciousness, deeper understanding of human and divine reality. Betrayal exacts a very dear, personal price, and when it can be resolved, it often takes much time and painful work. But to have been betrayed and to have forgiven is to emerge into new life, new consciousness, and new growth; it is to be initiated into adulthood.

Endnotes

1. Erik Erikson, *Young Man Luther* (New York: W.W. Norton, 1962), p. 118.
2. Erik Erikson, *Childhood and Society* (New York: W.W. Norton, 1963), p. 248.
3. Anthony Mello, S.J., *The Song of the Bird* (Chicago: Loyola University Press, 1983), p. 63.
4. See E.E. Whitehead, and J.D. Whitehead, *Christian Life Patterns: The Psychological Challenges and Religious Invitations of Adult Life* (New York: Doubleday, 1982).
5. See James Hillman, "Betrayal" in *Spring* (Dallas, Texas: Spring Publications, 1965): 57–76.

Raise your voice

Bernard J. Bush

Why anger? • Signs of anger • Accepting anger •
Sources of anger • Appropriate action •
A question of pride • Anger and God • Self-forgiveness

Reverend Bernard J. Bush, S.J., Ph.D. (cand.), is director of the House of Affirmation in Montara, California. A member of the California Province of the Society of Jesus who was ordained in 1965, Father Bush studied theology at Regis College, Willowdale, Ontario. He served as student chaplain at the University of San Francisco before assuming the post of spiritual director at the Jesuit theologate in Berkeley, California. From there he went to Boston State Hospital where he interned in pastoral psychology. In 1974 he joined the staff of the House of Affirmation and opened its Boston office. Father Bush has written numerous articles concerning spirituality and social justice, most notably in The Way. *He has been active in the directed retreat movement and has lectured on Ignatian spirituality, religious life, mental health, and social justice.*

It is sometimes necessary to speak loudly to get someone's attention or to show that we are serious. Volume is one of the ways that we verbally underline what we want to emphasize. Sometimes we even hear it said, "I have to shout to be heard around here!" Within the cosmos of our own inner life, I think our feelings act that way. They frequently have very important messages to give us. Thus our feelings represent in some way a shouting presence within that is calling our attention to something important going on that we must not ignore.

We know that there is always feeling activity going on within us, although we may not be consciously aware of it. Thus, in some sense we are always angry, always sad, always grieving, always responding sexually. These feelings can coexist and are an integral part of our life. At times under particular stress, provocation, or enticement one feeling may emerge demanding attention. So we say we are sad when sad feelings predominate and engage our attention. And so with anger. Identifying and mastering these emotions is a lifelong task to which God has set us by the very fact that we are human, and it is difficult work.

Why anger?

The feeling of anger arises in response to the perception of a threat. We judge that our well-being is under attack, or that we are somehow in danger. Our feelings call out to us that we need to make a response to this danger. Between the perception of danger and the response of anger, it seems we experience a sequence of stages. First there is a feeling of anxiety and uneasiness, then fear, and finally anger. Anger is the emotion that helps us mobilize to make a response to the perceived threat—fight or flight, as the saying goes.

Anger produces chemical changes within us. We know, for example, that when we are angry we become flushed. Our heart beats fast and we may begin to sweat. Our eyes dilate, our capillaries contract, and adrenalin begins to convert residual sugars into energy. The physiological changes that are taking place are preparing us to challenge some threat to our well-being, whether it be physical, emotional, or even spiritual. Anger is an essential part of our healthy defenses, and a signal that our will to live is functioning well. We want to go on living and so we want to ward off anything which would endanger that living.

Signs of anger

Becoming aware that we are angry requires sensitivity to those changes that take place in us. These physiological and emotional changes are the symptoms of anger. Yet it is possible to have all the symptoms, and yet not understand what they are telling us. Some people feel very calm when they are angry, maybe even icy calm. If so, then they need to recognize their own particular signs. Others are apparently not aware that they are feeling anything. In such cases, the angry energy is bottled up in their bodies where they develop various somatic problems, usually in the form of aches and pains. I am sure that many back, neck, shoulder, head, and stomach aches are the result of anger that has been buried alive.

Have you ever been driving down the highway and seen someone else driving in such a way that you just know the person is angry? The other car is being used like a weapon, and all you want to do is get out of the way. Impatience is a manifestation of anger, as are barbed and sarcastic comments.

Sometimes we meet people who smile all the time. Their perpetual smile, sometimes accompanied by a forced gentleness, feels false and unreal: it is a mask disguising something else, usually anger.

Anger can also be seen in the form of overreactions—that is, displaying more feeling than the situation warrants. In this case, anger has been displaced from the real object to another. Coming home from work and kicking the dog or slamming doors are examples of displacement of emotion. Extreme forms of moodiness, such as depression, withdrawal, the silent treatment, jealousy, and passive-aggressive behavior are all disguises of anger.

Resentments are the expressions of angers maintained over time, even a lifetime. Most of us carry some residual resentments over the hurts of the past. Many of them come from our family and upbringing. Perhaps we were trained to be nice little girls and boys; later we were expected to be perfect religious. All of that conditioning builds up resentments because we are not perfect and some of the time we are not even nice. If we have been forced or have forced ourselves to be what we are not, we will be resentful. Some say that unrecognized anger can be demonic. St. Paul tells us, "The sun must not go down on your wrath; do not give the devil a chance to work on you" (Eph. 5:26, 27).

When the sun does go down on your wrath, when you are harboring and nurturing anger, it continues to fester and grow. Andrew Lester in his book, *Coping With Your Anger: A Christian Guide,* says about this demonic quality of anger:

> ...unrecognized anger is an enemy to our spiritual sensitivity and to our ethical commitments. It can be a stumbling block to the redemptive process and sabotage the abundant life. This anger can be called demonic because it gives birth to hate instead of to nurturing love. It forsakes grace and pushes for punishment. Instead of working toward reconciliation, it breeds alienation. It shortcircuits the gift of forgiveness and promotes vengeance.[1]

I am suggesting that every time you and I run from anger or pretend that it does not exist we have collaborated with violence and sin; we have made ourselves more vulnerable to the destructively demonic. Thus the first step in the control of anger is awareness.

Accepting anger

The next step is acceptance. To do this we must simply become thoroughly convinced that feeling anger is not bad or sinful. Feelings are a part of the abundant life that God has given us, part of the energy that we have at our disposal. Anger is one of the vital ingredients that make us vibrant and real in our interactions with other people. No emotion is a sin.

Unfortunately, we do not always believe that it is not wrong to feel angry. Look at the language we sometimes use to disguise the fact that we are angry. We say that we are not angry, just irritated or upset. Or we are disgusted, frustrated, disappointed, nervous. The synonyms go on: fed up, peeved, bent out of shape, used, hurt, blue, down, and so on. There is something about the word "angry" that we consider unacceptable. We find substitute words for it that are a little more appealing or a bit more satisfactory or acceptable. We all remember William Blake's poem, "A Poison Tree."

> I was angry with my friend:
> I told my wrath, my wrath did end.
> I was angry with my foe:
> I told it not, my wrath did grow.
>
> And I water'd it in fears,
> Night and morning with my tears;
> And I sunned it with smiles,
> And with soft deceitful wiles.
>
> And it grew both day and night,
> Till it bore an apple bright;
> And my foe beheld it shine,
> And he knew that it was mine.
>
> And into my garden stole
> When the night had veil'd the pole:
> In the morning glad I see
> My foe outstretch'd beneath the tree.

Anger that is disguised or unaccepted poisons truth. A harboring of resentments becomes demonic and can lead to longstanding alienation.

Sources of anger

After accepting the anger we must then analyze it to find its source. We can generally tell from our knowledge of ourselves what some of those sources are. Frequently the problems that we have with anger began early in our lives. We may have experienced, for example, that anger was destructive of relationships. Perhaps our parents fought frequently and did not make up. If we have seen unresolved conflicts within the family, school, church, or even nation, then we grow up with a great fear of the power of the feeling. When that fear is translated into anger, we may find that we are angry at ourselves for feeling angry. Then we are ripe for depression. Yet anger is everywhere and within us at all times.

Religious life has its own particular set of stresses that generate anger and at the same time create difficulties in dealing with it. We religious are expected to be perpetually happy. We are supposed to be always caring, always solicitous about the welfare of other people. We need to be always cheerful and always available. We put on a facade that is never impatient. We are not supposed to set limits on our time: we are always and instantly completely available, never showing discomfort or any other disagreeable feelings. Yet our whole insides may be screaming out that we cannot face one more problem.

Repressed sexuality can generate a great deal of anger and resentment. Losses, too, are a source of anger. We have all heard of the stages of grieving; one of them is anger. If a friend moves away, or I myself move, I am going to go through a grieving process. Any change involves loss, and therefore anger. The change does not have to be a major upheaval or a dramatic loss like a death, either. All of life is transitions and processes and therefore losses and anger.

Anger is the appropriate response to offenses and injustices. Who does not feel some anger over the projections of the vast number of Ethiopians who are going to die of starvation this year?

More immediately, it is of utmost importance to analyze and understand the immediate sources of angry feelings. If someone steps on my toe, I get angry. That action is the source of my anger, the irritant. Yet most sources of anger are not so obvious. I may be in an argument with somebody and I am feeling angry, partly due to the argument, and partly due to something else. I may have been slighted or passed over; someone may have insulted me. We need to size up the provocations of the moment as well as the general background of our anger. When we have that degree of self-understanding we are in a position to evaluate whether the intensity of the feelings we are having is appropriate to the irritation.

Let me illustrate this point. If someone accidently steps on my foot, my anger would probably go up to one or two on a scale of ten. If someone comes along and deliberately stamps on my foot my anger may go up to seven or eight. If someone "puts me down" without reason, my emotion may escalate to ten, and a major provocation accompanied by an inner reservoir of anger could send me right off the scale. Now if someone accidently steps on my foot and my anger goes off the scale, I have overreacted. I may not have done or said anything about it yet, but I know that the feeling has gone way up, farther than it should have. It is then time to explore where the extra feeling is coming from. I may have a problem farther back in my life that I need to attend to.

Appropriate action

The next step to controlling anger is to take appropriate action. We need to understand that anger is great energy, a powerful motivator. It is hard to sit still when anger is all stirred up. When we are angry, we have a good deal of energy to channel appropriately. This word appropriate may cause some misunderstanding. It means simply that which is right for the occasion. Appropriate designates a proper balance, a fittingness, something which is proper, and is seen to be so by observers.

Appropriate action is controlled. It is not the wild, unleashed energy of a rage or a tantrum. The violent release of energy is inappropriate. Appropriate action is aimed at the proper target, and generally gets favorable results. It is not destructive, nor is it any of the whole wide spectrum of self-defeating behaviors such as sexual acting-out, drugs, or alcohol abuse. It respects proper authority and does not become antagonistic without cause.

Anger can be set aside without blocking, denying, or burying it in the dangerous ways we have been discussing. Sometimes it happens that we cannot express anger appropriately in a given situation. For example, if we are angry with someone who has just left the scene, it is of no help to kick the door. We will just hurt our foot or damage the door. We can, however, put our anger aside for the moment and resolve it when the person returns. We may have cooled down to the point where we can express it more appropriately under those delayed circumstances.

It is possible to be in a situation where it is too dangerous to express anger. This might be the case if we are dealing with someone who is highly volatile or violent, or perhaps with someone who has power over us. In this case we may have to "shelve" the anger and find another way to express it.

If the person with whom we are angry is dead, we have to find substitute ways of expressing ourselves. It is entirely possible and appropriate to tell our anger to a third party. This is not dumping on another, nor is it displacing the anger, but rather, talking it out. It is a way to dissipate the feelings, and can be adequate when more direct approaches are not available.

We know that exercise, creative activities, art, and athletics are generally safe substitutions for expressing anger. They are ways of draining off the immediate energy but do not, however, deal with the source. The anger thus evaporated can return later in the form of lingering resentments. These alternative means of handling anger are perfectly acceptable as long as we know what we are doing. However, if working off anger in these ways is the only means we have, we will find them unsatisfactory in the long run, since we have not dealt with the sources of the anger.

A question of pride

When we are working with these powerful feelings we are faced with some of our limitations. The first step is always to look at ourselves before we look at the provocation. If we keep looking at the source outside ourselves we are greatly tempted to blame or scapegoat others for our feelings. Yet no one can make another angry. A person can do a variety of provoking things, but our anger is always our anger. It is our response to someone else's behavior. We own it. The provoker of feelings has some responsibility for the responses his or her behavior draws, but not entirely. We use this inaccurate language all the time: "He made me so mad!" Rather, he did something irritating, and I got angry in response. Anger is always a sign of some connection; if we do not care we do not get angry.

I would like to suggest that there is another problem here and it involves the struggle with our pride. There is within most of us a need to look good and to justify ourselves. In dealing with anger pride takes the form of self-righteousness and indignation. Perhaps we "pull rank" when we feel threatened or our argument is weak. This indignation tells us we are virtuous to feel and act this way. It is a heady and powerful feeling; it is also probably wrong.

Anger and God

If we take a spiritual perspective on our feelings, we find another source of strength which enables us to remove ourselves from the immediate enmeshment and confusion. It is a way of shining a different colored light on the situation so that we see it from an altered viewpoint, a greater distance. We can be more objective than when we react spontaneously.

Because there are inevitable losses in our life, anger is always going to be part of our existential condition. It reminds us of our mortality and our limitations. It provides opportunities for humility and a way of realizing that we are not God. Anger can be a strong reminder that we need to raise our voice in prayer, to ask God for light and enlightenment to temper the heat and the confusion.

Anger provides us with the opportunity to reach out in reconciliation in the midst of a strife that frequently leads to estrangement and alienation. ". . . leave your gift at the altar, go first to be reconciled with your brother, and then come and offer your gift" (Matt. 5:24). Christ came to reconcile the world to God in his own person, and it is our task to carry on that ministry of reconciliation.

To nurture and foster the anger that leads to hatred is sinful. We can raise our voices to unite our concerns with God's concerns. Even though there are many things awry in the world, we know that God wills justice and peace, mercy, harmony, and compassion. Anger in these areas can be joined to God's own. We know that Jesus was angry when he saw religion misused. These feelings can be a message from God to direct our attention to something of great value and importance. God's message cannot and should not be ignored.

Self-forgiveness

We need to be gentle with ourselves. Take the golden rule and reverse it: we need to treat ourselves as we treat other people. Most of us, most of the time, are pretty decent and compassionate with others. But how are we with ourselves? How much of our anger, violence, hostility, and even hatred gets turned back on ourselves? How much reconciling must we do with our own battered psyche? We know that no one batters us for the most part as we batter ourselves. Adrian van Kaam in an article, "Anger and the Gentle Life," states:

> I can be gentle with myself if I can experience myself simultaneously as precious, fragile, and vulnerable. I know from daily experience that I am not always faithful to myself. Many times I feel disappointed in myself, experiencing how I prevent my better self from flourishing.... Most people are not inclined to feel gently towards this disappointing self because they do not look with love at the precious person they are called to be.... Self-condemnation does not give rise to a gentle approach to themselves. At such moments I want to whip myself into shape. I feel that I have to discipline myself mercilessly, forgetting that I may harm my finer sensitivities and silence my better self.... Many people see themselves only as bad, undisciplined, lazy, and willfully resisting improvement. There is undoubtedly some truth in all of this. But it is not the whole truth....
>
> A first step to inner gentleness is thus to gratefully love myself as a unique gift and to admit and accept my weakness which makes me the fragile vessel of this treasure. Gentleness with self is possible only when I recognize and "own" also the vulnerability of the treasure I am. I must be able to look at myself with a forgiving eye.[2]

We would never willingly smash an object that is precious, vulnerable, and valuable. When we pick up one of those delicate painted eggs we handle it carefully. If we hold a glass that is very thin and fragile we do not start tossing it around to see how strong it is. Why do we not treat ourselves with the same consideration? Simply put, we must learn to look at ourselves with a forgiving eye.

Anger, then, is a good sign that we are alive and healthy. We can listen to our anger as a voice from within calling our attention to important things. We can then use it to give our own voice strength and power, not in hostility and violent shouting, but in insistent prayer that draws God's attention to something that needs to be attended to.

Endnotes

1. Andrew D. Lester, *Coping With Your Anger* (Philadelphia: Westminster Press, 1983), p. 54.
2. Adrian van Kaam, "Anger and the Gentle Life," *Humanitas* 12 (May 1976): 258–259.

"Be like the birds of the air and the lilies of the field...."

A spiritual approach to healing the wounds of anger and resentment

Craig F. Evans

Anger: a figment of our imagination • Focus on the Now •
The power of the mind • Undoing the false self •
Changing our way of thinking • Learning forgiveness •
Letting go of resentment • Pride

Craig F. Evans, L.I.C.S.W., is a psychotherapist at the House of Affirmation in Boston, Massachusetts. He received a bachelor's degree from Marist College, Poughkeepsie, New York, and a master's degree in social work from West Virginia University, Morgantown, West Virginia. Mr. Evans is a member of the Academy of Certified Social Workers and the National Association of Social Workers, as well as a trustee of the Vermont Academy of Arts and Sciences.

Since I first expressed an interest in participating in this symposium I have found my direction and attention moving from the strictly psychological level to a more spiritual one—a move that has felt altogether comfortable and right, and in some ways, exciting. Let me emphasize that what I am presenting is a belief system that can lead to certain experiences. Without question, this belief system is based on an ideal—a Christian ideal founded on Jesus' teachings and life. It has its roots in an internal experience, not an external one, and it is highly individual, with the common denominator of a single goal. It is a belief that I have been growing into over a significant period of time. This belief is something I want to share with you and something I would invite you to consider for yourself. You might say that I am presenting you with a challenge.

Anger: a figment of our imagination

Essentially, I would like to say that anger, like sex, is not all it is cracked up to be. You or I would never know that if we were exposed only to the predominant psychological thinking on this matter. Anger has been charged with being the cause of almost any malady, from obesity to depression, from high blood pressure to hormonal imbalance. It has been viewed as the motivating force behind a variety of behaviors, as well as the result of some of those behaviors. Anger has been thrown together with aggression and the two made simultaneous in occurrence and mutual in origin.

There are those who feel anger has its origin exclusively in biology; others who view it as strictly instinctual; still others who see it only on the affective plane. Some consider it a motivation for challenging the injustices of life.

Anger has been attributed to the unconscious as well as the conscious. It has even been reified to the extent that individuals claim it resides in areas of the body—the back of the neck, the guts, the lungs, the shoulders, the big toe, and so on. There are those who argue that one gender deals with anger better than the other, or that one gender has more reason for being angry.

Carol Tavris, in her book, *Anger, the Misunderstood Emotion*, undertakes a monumental task of synthesizing the significant research done over the past century on this topic and the major theoretical stances of psychology.[1] I refer you to her excellent book rather than try to summarize it. Without doubt, there is still much to be learned about anger and other emotions.

To return to my first point—anger is not all it is cracked up to be. I would even say that it is a figment of our imagination. If that is the case, why all the hullabaloo—books, symposia, therapies? This symposium provides an opportunity for all of us to understand better something that has been given "bad press" for a long time. We have a chance to look at anger not only from a psychological perspective, but also in relation to our individual spiritual journeys.

I have always been uncomfortable with the emphasis of some clinicians, trained and untrained, on "expressing your anger," particularly when the same individual who learns to rant and rave is not encouraged to work at expressing other emotions with equal attention and seriousness. I do not believe that anger is the root of all problems, and I would like to explain what I am coming to believe.

Focus on the Now

We have been given everything we need to be happy now.[2] Contentedness or serenity found in the present moment enables us to extend peace to others as well as to experience the inner peace of Christ. Anxiety, on the other hand, the only alternative to trusting what is happening, is a state of immobilization caused by our focusing on what we believe cannot be changed: on what is over, or on what has not occurred.[3]

We allow ourselves to be pressured from both sides: guilt for things done or things undone, and the opposing side of guilt that holds other people or circumstances responsible for our unhappiness. I am talking here about a belief system set up to work destructively because it promotes guilt and anger, and blocks out the possibility of spiritual healing through forgiveness and relationships. Guilt, fear, anger, and remorse are all opposites of love; these opposites cannot co-exist.

In order to see the world differently, we must be willing to change our belief system: to let go of the past, focus on our sense of the present moment (what I call the Now), and erase from our minds the fear of the future.

Jesus focused on the present with simplicity and contentedness. He taught his disciples that regardless of the appearance of any present condition or event, God is working to bring about good—instances that Ken Wapnick refers to as "holy encounters" in *Forgiveness and Jesus*.[4] In John 9:2, the disciples ask Jesus about the blind man: "Rabbi, who sinned, this man or his parents, that he was born blind?" Jesus answered, "It was not that this man sinned, or his parents, but that the works of God might be made manifest in him."

This new perception, this focus on the Now, can lead us to the recognition and acceptance that we are not separated, but have always been joined with one another, with the Christ, and with God. The essence of our being is love. We all have everything we need now; we just have to grow into that awareness. We have only this moment in which to become aware; the past is past, and the future is not yet.

The power of the mind

Would it disturb you if I told you that we live in our minds, that basically we make our own world because what happens to us is neutral in and of itself? Let me offer a simple example and then consider this concept in a little more detail.

Recently I attended a very good workshop. During one of the sessions, my mind wandered to this presentation. I began to think about the positioning of my presentation, what I have come to call "bringing up the rear." I focused on the fact that I would be addressing these hundreds of people right after lunch, the best time for the traditional siesta—the implication being that I was the sedative.

Then I saw the light! I realized that I choose how I perceive this moment, and projecting ahead to it would only cripple my chance to experience it as a "holy encounter." In addition, I was avoiding the present moment by focusing on the fears of the future. I am free today to approach this moment in a Spirit-filled way, extending outwardly God's love which is my essence, and receiving it back with gratitude. I can only do this if I let go of the guilt of the past and the fear of the future.

Another example of this frame of reference system which is even more to the point of anger is presented by Carol Tavris. There is an old sociological theory that people crowded together cause various forms of social pathology, like juvenile delinquency, crime, VD, and prostitution, according to the degree of crowdedness. Tavris blasts this theory with various other scientific studies that indicate that it is not the crowding itself that creates anger and subsequent social pathos, but one's perceptions about the crowd. The mere presence of many other people is indeed arousing, but whether that arousal is transformed into pleasure or anger depends less on whether you are crowded than on whether you feel crowded. If I have been anxious in front of large groups in the past, I still have the freedom at this moment to choose how I will perceive being in front of this large audience. I can let the past slip away or I can cling to the past and the resulting fear of the future.

Arousal is one of the key words here, for there are choices as to how one deals with arousal. The first step is accepting the existence of the arousal, taking the responsibility for its presence, and choice of the corresponding emotion. This wisdom is implied in the ancient adage, "Know thyself."

Frequently the response to any suggestion of taking control of the way one thinks goes something like this: "I can't seem to let go of those thoughts and feelings, no matter how hard I try." There is a simple mental principle available to each of us: the best way to stop thinking about something is to think about something else. This principle is based on the fact that we can think about only one thing at a time. Such an ideal, of course, implies a desire and a willingness to give up the almost hypnotic state of reveling in thoughts of guilt and anger over past events, or thoughts that comfort us by allowing us to feel sorry for ourselves. Striving for this ideal of taking more positive control implies a willingness to clean out what I often refer to as "the can of worms"—resentment, hatred, blaming of others, self-pity, bitterness, inward anger, and other self-indulgences. "When we cherish grievances, we allow our mind to be fed by fear and we become imprisoned by these distortions."[5]

I am saying, then, that what we experience in the world is our state of mind projected outwardly. If our state of mind is one of well-being, love, and inner peace, that is what we will project, and that is what we will experience. If our state of mind is one filled with doubt and fear, we will project that state outwardly, and that will be our experience. Summarily, then, there are only two emotions: love and fear. Love is our essence, for if we believe that God is love and we are made in his image and likeness, then we too are love. "Fear is something made up by our mind" and is therefore unreal.[6]

Ram Dass, who was once called Richard Alpert, a colleague of Timothy Leary and a trained psychologist, tells the story about his guru in India suggesting that he return to the States. Ram Dass felt afraid, and when questioned by his guru as to what frightened him, responded, "Well, what else can I be afraid of but my own impurities? I'm afraid that I'm going to get lost again in my own desires." His guru walked over to him, looked him up and down, and said, "I don't see any impurities." Ram Dass thus deepened his understanding of the nature of the work with other human beings. That work involves looking behind another individual's personality and body—beyond even the thinking mind—to the place where we are the manifestation of love. It is looking for God in every being.[7] Implicit in this process is the belief that each of us can experience the love of God that is our essence.

Ram Dass goes on to describe the ability of a saint to walk through the busiest part of a large city, and experience it as the peacefulness of the country. If a handsome man or beautiful woman walks in front of the saint, the saint notices that person, and recognizes his or her own reaction, but does not get lost in these reactions nor go off center.

This story reminded me of a similar one related in Furlong's biography of Thomas Merton. She discusses how Merton, who was quite candid about his difficulties with chastity early in his religious life, arrived at the ability to look at a beautiful woman and not be distracted and made anxious. He learned that he could appreciate her beauty in the moment, and his own appreciation of that beauty registered by his arousal, and leave it at that. He chose how he would deal with the arousal and what emotion was appropriate at the present moment.[8]

What I am saying about control is not new, at least to some of us. The wisdom of the serenity prayer of Alcoholics Anonymous says it clearly: "Accept the things we cannot change, change the things we can, and know the difference." It is a prayer calling for serenity, courage, and wisdom. I believe that we do have control over how we think about things, how we allow ourselves to see the world, which is totally neutral in its illusion. We do not have control over others; other people do not have to change for us to experience peace of mind and serenity.

Undoing the false self

So how does all this apply to anger? Ram Dass says, "Anger is always an attachment to a model of where you wish you were other than where you are, or how you wish it were other than the way it is. The minute you stop having models, the anger goes."[9] And we do have models! There are models for masculinity and femininity; there are models for how to dress, how to walk, how to talk, what to read, how to be a saint, and how to be the perfect religious or cleric. The models that we incorporate into our belief system—which are more appropriately labeled misperceptions—are projected onto the world and made into our reality. They have nothing to do with our essence as experienced in the present moment, but rather reflect the guilt of the past and fears of the future. Those misperceptions can only be undone in the Now, in the present moment, the moment of choice. The undoing is accomplished through letting go of whatever we think other people have done to us, or whatever we think we have done to them. In doing this, we are liberated to experience the present without the need to re-enact the past or project into the fears of the future.

Ken Wapnick refers to the ego as the false self—that is, the self that we have constructed as the replacement for the self that God created in his image and likeness. The prototype for the self is Adam, who sought to change what his Father had created as perfect. We understand then that Adam left the unified state of perfect love with God, and the God of love was transformed into a God of fear, a God who seeks to avenge and to punish his children for their crime of separation.

The separated ego thereby seeks to support itself through perpetuating the guilt of the past for things done and undone.[10] The peace that is our natural inheritance is turned into a state of terror and anxiety; fear intensifies the guilt, and subsequently, the guilt intensifies the fear. We come to believe in this enormous guilt and even accept it as if it reflected our true reality. We defend against it by projecting it onto someone or something external to us, and then struggle to continue to keep it projected outside ourselves.

The only way we can liberate ourselves from this projection and sense of separation is to allow our true essence to shine. John speaks of "perfect love casting out fear" (1 John 4:19). We can choose to experience that phenomenon when we look within and beyond our own fear and guilt and find the Christ who is our true self. If we are to become consciously aware of our true identity, of our perfect union with God, the ego—the false self—must be undone. I believe this is the journey each of us is making, with a common goal of union with our loving Father.

Those of you who are familiar with the fellowship of Alcoholics Anonymous have probably already begun to recognize a similarity between what I am presenting and the steps and traditions of the AA program. That program works so well for so many because it is based on essential principles of acceptance of one's condition, which includes a powerlessness and a surrender to a higher power. Through the surrender process, individuals choose to let go of the past and the future and accept the Now. They choose to liberate themselves from their ego and to correct their distorted thinking with fresh insight and guidance from others in the program, the written counsel of the program, and the energy released through the actual fellowship that happens in those meeting halls. I firmly believe that what makes the program work is the grace-filled moments of that fellowship—grace that enables the individuals to look honestly at themselves and realize their own goodness, and to let go of the old distortions that have kept them in a hornet's nest of shame, guilt, and fear for years.

One of the primary distortions cherished by alcoholic persons is that they are somehow not responsible for their drinking. All is projected onto others—the guilt, the remorse, the shame, and the fear. Part of their recovery process is not only being able to rid themselves of this primary distortion, but also to be able to "turn over" the past, and to learn to live in the present moment. The steps of the fellowship are designed to help the men and women who have chosen to begin their recovery to do it thoroughly and explicitly. This process allows them the beginnings of true kinship with other people, and with their higher power. The love that was blocked by anger and guilt is freed, and it is that loving energy that they can choose to experience in the fellowship, when they are ready to recognize it as their own true essence.

Changing our way of thinking

Let us talk more practically about how we can make changes in our way of thinking, in our minds, since we must learn to think differently if we are to change things in our lives. Gerald Jampolsky, a psychiatrist from the West Coast, suggests five basic questions to be asked in all circumstances:

- Do I choose to experience peace of mind, or do I choose to experience conflict?
- Do I choose to experience love or fear?
- Do I choose to be a love-finder or a fault-finder?
- Do I choose to be a love-giver or a love-seeker?
- Is this communication (verbal or nonverbal) loving to the other person, and is it loving to me?[11]

Through these five questions, we can focus our mental and spiritual energy away from the ego elements of fear and guilt which lend themselves to attack and separation, and in the direction of forgiveness, and loving and healing relationships that reflect our true nature. We have that choice. The first step toward forgiveness and healing is to change our way of thinking.

If we are able to free ourselves of the pride that keeps us believing that others are responsible for our unhappiness, we are liberated to forgive peacefully with a totality that lets go of the superior attitude that often accompanies forgiveness. Ram Dass speaks of the incredible mountain, pride, that pushes us to "save face" in the name of forgiveness.[12] Jesus taught that forgiveness must be a total experience, that anger and guilt must be given up, and we must love everyone. "When we feel anger, or disappointment, or experience hatred or condemnation, it is because we have not identified with our true nature."[13]

Our problem then is in us, and not in the external world, which after all is but a projection of ourselves. If we can recognize who we truly are—the love that is our essence—and as a result feel the security and strength of God in us, then our perceptions will reflect peace, love, and serenity. Faith in Jesus, the teacher of love, overcomes fear through personal affirmations. The transformation of our minds is the freeing element in our pursuit of serenity. We have been given everything we need to be happy.

Learning forgiveness

I spoke earlier of what Ken Wapnick calls the "holy encounter"—that encounter that holds out to us the potential for forgiveness and union with God through the Spirit. "Every event in our lives is another opportunity to learn the Spirit's single lesson of forgiveness."[14] By seeing the God in other individuals, we become better able to see and experience our own true self. That forgiveness enables us to form healing relationships in the spirit of love. Guilt and fear, the cornerstones of the ego, have no room in healing relationships. This is the ultimate in At-One-Ment which Jampolsky speaks of, the unity of love that is our true nature and essence.

Of course, we are also familiar with all the exceptions we try to make to the teaching of Jesus: those individuals whom we think we really cannot forgive, or those special instances when we believe it would be unreasonable to expect us to look for love in the situation or person. Once again that enormous mountain, pride, encourages us to save face and restrict ourselves with guilt and fear, to attack rather than heal, to separate rather than join.

I would like to share another exercise that might prove helpful. It comes from a short article by Eugene Sorenson published in a Unity Easter pamphlet. Sorenson suggests the following formula as being one effective way to help change our thinking, and to express to others what it is that we want to express.

Upon waking in the morning, consider the attitudes of mind and heart that you wish to extend to the people with whom you will come in contact. Project love, joy, peace, and harmony on the screen of your mind. Then, in front of a mirror, put these qualities and attitudes in your bodily stance, and especially your facial expression. Take note of how you feel inside, how you look on the outside. Throughout your day, the moment you are aware that you are not showing on the outside the way you felt earlier on the inside, reject the false picture or distortion you are portraying, and accept once again your original radiant expression—that of your true nature.[15]

Striving for the outer expression of such an attitude will foster happy, satisfying relationships, and a sense of peace and calm that will promote harmony and order in all that you do. Of course, it also involves a lot of work, and before undertaking such an exercise, you must believe that we are meant to live happy, fulfilling lives, and that our God is indeed a God of love. It is ultimately that principle of which we must remind ourselves each day.

The teachings of Jesus constantly remind us that we choose how we will think about things, and as a result, how we will act. In the parables, Jesus teaches over and over that we have free choice—as sowers choosing to sow on fertile or barren ground, as virgins preparing the lamps for the bridegroom or leaving them empty, or as trees producing sound or inferior fruit. In Mark, Jesus speaks even more explicitly: "Can you not see that whatever goes into a man from the outside cannot make him unclean? It is what comes out of man that makes him unclean. For it is from within, from men's hearts, that evil intentions emerge" (Mark 7:15-16). Perhaps the most significant of all the teachings of Jesus is found in his Sermon on the Mount, in which he presents us with the beatitudes, a clear and radical message. Equally radical is the love Jesus expresses to us in John: "Peace I leave to you, my peace I give to you—a peace this world cannot give, this is my gift to you" (John 14:27).

Letting go of resentment

Much of this discussion has focused on the need for letting go of resentments, anger, and guilt from the past. I would like to take a few minutes to focus on another simple exercise. Accepting the fact that we must let go of resentments is one thing—having an effective way of doing that is another. Carl and Stephanie Simenton in their book, *Getting Well Again*, outline one such way. Essentially, the process in this exercise is to become aware of an individual for whom you harbor resentment, and to try to picture good things happening to that person. The Simentons suggest the following experiences as targets for this process: "nursing an old hurt; reliving a distressing episode; thinking over and over what you should have done or said; recalling another person's reprehensible behavior."

The exercise should be followed in this way.

1. Sit in a comfortable chair, feet flat on the floor, eyes closed.

2. If you feel tense or distracted, use a relaxation process. (I would recommend a simple deep breathing, using a count of eight for inhaling and again for exhaling, over a period of about three minutes.)

3. Create a clear picture in your mind of the person toward whom you feel resentment.

4. Picture good things happening to that person. See him or her receiving love or attention or money, whatever you believe that person would see as a good thing. (See yourself and the other person as both filled with inner peace and love.)

5. Be aware of your own reactions. If you have difficulty seeing good things happening to the person, it is a natural reaction. It will become easier with practice.

6. Think about the role you may have played in the stressful scene and how you might re-interpret the event and the other person's behavior. Imagine how the situation might look from the other person's point of view.

7. Be aware of how much more relaxed, less resentful you feel. Tell yourself you will carry this new understanding with you.

8. Now open your eyes and resume your usual activities.[16]

Do not expect instant release with this exercise. Rather, expect to have to work with it as much as is necessary in order to let go of those painful grievances that keep you locked in the ego.

Pride

Finally, I would like to talk briefly about pride, "the enormous mountain." Pride is based on our guilt and fear; it is our own denial of the love that we are, and it is the liability that keeps us separated from forgiving relationships. Wapnick says that "without our physical presence, and our desire and willingness to join with [Jesus], the world could not hear [his] words, nor see his ever-loving way of forgiving."[17]

To practice the Word of God as Jesus taught us means to overcome our own denial of who we are, to love our neighbor as we love ourselves, and to put our faith in our Father. We have been taught by Jesus that anything that we ask for in his name we will receive, for together with him we reflect the creation of our Father and his everlasting love. That was Jesus' final prayer: "Father, may they be one in us, as you are in me, and I am in you, so that the world may believe it was you who sent me. I have made your name known to them and will continue to make it known, so that the love with which you loved me may be in them, and so that I may be in them" (John 17:21, 26).

Conclusion

I would like to end by sharing a brief reflection with you that I have found filled with the Spirit. It is from a series prepared by Unity for the 1984 Lenten season. This particular meditation was intended for the fifth day of Lent.

> You have often been told or perhaps you have read the words: *Watch your step.*
> This is important, of course, but more needful is the caution to watch your thoughts.
> Your thoughts create your steps.
> Your thoughts create your future.
> Your thoughts create your destiny.
> Your thoughts may
> chain you,
> harm you,
> and imprison you.
> Or
> they may free,
> enrich,
> and bless you.

As a person thinks, so is he. His life is in relation to his thought, always.

Thought is the tool you use to carve your future.

You have sown seeds often enough in your garden to know that the seed is true to itself. You do not gather marigolds if you plant petunias.

If you sow undisciplined, negative thoughts, you cannot reap serenity and feelings of spiritual peace.

By all means, watch your step, but most importantly, watch your thoughts.

Endnotes

The inspirational works of several individuals have aided me in preparing this paper. *A Course in Miracles*, published by the Foundation for Inner Peace, is the basis for the reflections of Gerald G. Jampolsky, M.D. and Kenneth Wapnick, Ph.D. I am thankful to these two authors, and to the many authors associated with Unity Publications, Unity Village, Missouri.

1. Carol Tavris, *Anger: The Misunderstood Emotion* (New York: Simon and Schuster, 1982).

2. Gerald G. Jampolsky, *Love is Letting Go of Fear* (New York: Bantam Books, 1979), p. 7.

3. Jampolsky, p. 8.

4. Kenneth Wapnick, *Forgiveness and Jesus* (Farmingdale, N.Y.: Coleman Graphics, 1983).

5. Jampolsky, p. 65.

6. Jampolsky, p. 43.

7. Baba Ram Dass, "What Do We Say of the Self to Be Realized?" *Cross Currents* 24, 2-3: 286.

8. Monica Furlong, *Merton: A Biography* (New York: Harper and Row, 1980).

9. Baba Ram Dass, p. 283.

10. Wapnick, *Forgiveness and Jesus*, p. 19.

11. Jampolsky, p. 37.

12. Baba Ram Dass, p. 285.

13. Kenneth Wapnick, *Christian Psychology in "A Course in Miracles"* (Farmingdale, N.Y.: Coleman Graphics, 1978), p. 12.

14. Wapnick, *Christian Psychology*, p. 15.

15. Eugene Sorenson, "Shine Forth the Truth of You," *Take the Wings of the Morning* (Unity Village, Missouri: Unity Publications), p. 51.

16. O. Carl and Stephanie Matthews-Simonton and James L. Creighton, *Getting Well Again* (New York: Bantam Books, 1978), p. 152.

17. Wapnick, *Forgiveness and Jesus*, p. 298.

The anger of nothingness:
An access to intimacy

Thomas J. Tyrrell

What is this thing called anger? • The experience of
nothingness • A proclamation of meaning • Creative
response to a meaningless life • The call to authenticity •
The void within • The need for others • Witnessing to the sacred

*Thomas J. Tyrrell, Ph.D., is assistant director of the House of Affirmation in
Clearwater, Florida. He received a master's degree from George Peabody
College, Nashville, Tennessee; and a doctorate in clinical psychology from
Duquesne University, Pittsburgh, Pennsylvania. In each of these programs
he minored in philosophy. He has taught the psychology of personality
development at both the undergraduate and graduate levels. He is a fellow in
the National Institute of Mental Health and the Eastern Pennsylvania Psy-
chiatric Institute. Dr. Tyrrell, a member of the American Psychological
Association and the Florida Psychological Association, has lectured
throughout the United States and Canada and is the author of the book*
Urgent Longings, *a study of infatuation and intimacy. He is recognized for
his work on interpersonal intimacy and is currently writing a book on that
topic.*

Michael Novak, in his book *The Experience of Nothingness,*
writes that we live a fragile existence in a universe of darkness and
chaos.[1] There is hope, however; he and authors such as William Kraft
believe that it is through the various stages and experiences of
suffering—of nothingness—that we are able to discern, find meaning,
and undergo a transformation to greater authenticity and happiness.[2]
Modern and contemporary philosophers such as Søren Kierke-
gaard, Karl Jaspers, and Martin Heidegger accept the fact of
"nothingness" and address both its mode of expression and its role in
human emergence.[3,4] They encourage us to be a people of fidelity, to
confront, enter, undergo negative experiences, and be transformed.
Indeed, Jaspers is most pointed in his advice. He tells us, in effect,
that the being and the becoming of human existence are realized in
the authenticating movement, wherein we decide whether to sink into
nothingness or affirm our existence.[5]

When faced with the negative experiences of misunderstanding, resentment, or injustice, we may formulate Jaspers's insight through the following questions: does the pain of this negative experience stop our personal, spiritual emergence? Do we sink into the sadness of disappointment, the anger of injustice, the despair of failure? Do we surrender to nihilism? If we live from the belief that there is nothing beyond nothingness, we will not be open to negative experiences. We will act out of faith in our own power and self-sufficiency, and we will strive to distance ourselves from the experience.

From the guidance and encouragement of philosophers such as Jaspers, we draw hope. When faced with the darkness and pain of suffering we are invited to stand in optimism. We are invited to believe that the darkness can be entered, the pain endured; that in and through the suffering we can be recreated. We are invited to participate more fully in life, all of life. We are taught that the despair of failure, the sadness of disappointment, the anger of injustice offer the possibility of rebirth into authenticity.

Through the disciplines of philosophical anthropology, existential psychology, and contemporary theology we learn to see the human spirit as dynamic, unfolding, and revealed through experience. We find that this dynamic unfolding manifests itself in an ever changing mystery of integrating and disintegrating life forces. The interplay of these two forces is glaringly visible when we are confronted with negative experiences. In the face of anxiety, despair, anger, we find ourselves caught in a tension of possibilities. And so we must choose. Do we stand in optimism, or do we falsify our existence? Do we hide our anxiety, sadness, anger behind a mask of denial? Do we blame ourselves or others for the misfortune that has befallen us? Or do we enter the experience, acknowledging that we are afraid, but knowing in our hearts that we carry a burning desire to walk with the One from whom all justice is drawn?

What is this thing called anger?

Carol Tavris calls anger "the misunderstood emotion." Through her study of anger we learn there is a school of thought that sees unexpressed anger as gathering force, acting on our will, and robbing us of our freedom and vitality.[6] This school of thought argues that unless we give vent to those feelings we will fill up like a pressure cooker. Our bodies, unable to withstand the stress, eventually break down; we experience ulcers, hypertension, sexual dysfunction, alcoholism, even acne.[7]

Tavris, in her review of the literature, finds little evidence to substantiate what she and others refer to as the "ventilationist" perspective. She does, however, point to a number of studies that seem to contradict it. She notes that in those moments when patience with self or other has eroded; when our defenses are lowered by fatigue, wounded pride, or just plain exasperation; when we give vent to negative feelings, especially anger, we are often immediately consumed by confusion, anxiety, guilt, and self-doubt. Rather than being more free, we find ourselves more inhibited than before.[8]

What is this "thing" called "anger"? How are we to understand its effect upon our lives? Does it promote or inhibit the dynamic unfolding and emergence of the human spirit? To respond to these questions requires admitting to our consciousness the fact, or at least the possibility, that we can be angry. In so doing we are also admitting to the absurdity, loss of meaning, confusion, and self-doubt that flow from an angry situation. Thus, our approach will be to view the non-sense of anger: that is, we will view anger as a lived experience— one in which there are intertwined both integrating and disintegrating life forces. Further, we will view anger as an experience which does not reflect an act of bad faith when suppressed or expressed, but does promote loss of authenticity when not acknowledged.

Focusing on the "what" of anger, we ask that its existence be acknowledged as fact or possibility, in self or other—that we not falsify the possibilities for human emergence by denying the lived experience of anger in self or other. We also ask that we stand in courage and hope, and listen to the deeper message that might be given in and through all human experiences, including that of anger.

As with all reflective paradigms, personal or theoretical, we make certain assumptions. The first is that anger is not a "thing" that lies within the human breast like a dormant volcano waiting to go off and spill over onto any innocent passerby. Rather, we view anger as situated. That is, it emerges from within a context created by the event and the participants; what emerges and our response are co-constituted events. This presumption suggests that the angry emotion of self or other arises in response to the implicit and explicit realities experienced by the participants. In other words, this assumption holds that angry feelings are a meaningful response to a situation constituted by human intention. As such, the experience of anger, like all human experiences, needs the clarifying illumination of a discerning will in order for us to make sense of it, to find its meaning. Second, it calls upon us to assume responsibility for the angry feelings and the situation which gave rise to those feelings. Witness the following example.

"You must be very angry that your wife died."

"No, I am just rather sad and confused."

"But she did abandon you."

"I suppose, but I'm really not angry, just sad."

"I mean, after all, you now have to raise those seven small children yourself."

"I . . . I'm really not angry."

"You know, the culture is so unfair to single parents with children and she's gone."

"I am not angry!"

"Then why are you shouting?"

Here the act of discernment makes the implicit reality immediately transparent. The source of the angry response is easily traced: it is clearly the insensitivity and injustice of the other's judgment. Here we see anger as an appropriate, healthy response to interpersonal injustice. The bereaved, however, could have behaved differently and not revealed his angry feelings. He could have chosen to be inauthentic and go along with the other, or he could have hidden behind a mask of smiling denial; he could have flown into a murderous rage or withdrawn into suicidal despair. In the drama of human life, these are but a few possibilities.

But we must also acknowledge that the angry widower, in a moment of vulnerability, reacted to the judgment of another. The well-meaning friend was unjust, but the young widower will also have to assume responsibility for his loss of gentleness.

In this presentation we will touch briefly upon the ordinary as well as the pathological response to the experience of anger. But we will make the claim that while anger is generally a response to injustice, it usually arises from a unique situation. Thus, our response depends upon our unique personal formation story.

Adrian van Kaam indicates that culture, subculture, environment, history, temperament, and family are but some of the formative features that shape the experience, meaning, and response of an anger-promoting situation.[9] Witness, for example, the cultural aspect of formation: to a Japanese male, an overtly angry response to injustice would mean loss of face, whereas the opposite would be true for a Saudi Arabian male. The same holds true for other aspects of human formation, since the situation and response will be unique, formed by people interacting with and within specialized worlds of meaning.

Therefore, ordinary anger and our unique response to it may not be necessary for the emergence and unfolding of human existence. The experience of nothingness, however, which all of us will undergo, is essential for our personal growth and transformation into authenticity.

We can express or mortify the experience of ordinary anger. Witness the final moments of Sir Thomas More, as captured in Robert Bolt's play, *A Man for All Seasons*. More is about to lose his head for acting with integrity. Certainly anger would be a reasonable response. Instead, More, in an act of sensitivity to his executioner, says, "Friend, be not afraid of your office. You send me to God."[10]

And yet, why should More be angry? As his later canonization would seem to indicate, his final moments do not signify that he had drifted into a spiritless existence. If, however, More had been inauthentic to self, other, and most especially to the sacred, if in the course of his life he had said no to the anger of nothingness, he would have refused an experience of creative aggression. This aggression serves the transforming power of love and destroys the false, the inauthentic. Such an aggression is in the service of the Authentic Being himself, denouncing the vendors in his father's house.

Before proceeding we make one additional comment about our approach: the focus will be the nothingness of creative anger. However, this emotion is certainly not the only one that can reveal the experience of creative suffering. Next, we will confine our remarks on anger to the experience of nothingness in relation to self, other, and the sacred. Finally, our remarks will be within the context of relationship.

The experience of nothingness

Consider the following painful moment in the life of a forty-two-year-old woman religious. She was director of religious education in a large suburban parish with ten years of experience and master's degrees in both psychology and religious education. At the time, she was undergoing therapy, having initiated the process because of her feelings of confusion, sadness, and self-doubt:

> I awoke one morning at the usual time, dressed, went to chapel for morning prayer and eucharist. Suddenly, I became aware that as I uttered my morning prayers, my usually placid mood began to change. The words I spoke were flat, lifeless, boring. I suddenly got very impatient with the sister who was leading us in prayer. I wanted to shout, "For God's sake, put some life into it." I was a bit frightened by the intensity of my feelings, but even in my fear, I still wanted to lash out. I was so frustrated by her boring, empty, meaningless recital. As liturgy continued, I got even more irritated by the listless response of those around me. Everyone seemed so lifeless, mechanical. And when the services ended, angry feelings were sparked once more by the way everyone left chapel, so self-absorbed, so caught up in their private little worlds. I wanted to cry and scream at the same time. I was so sad, yet I wanted to shake everyone and tell them to wake up!
>
> The experience continued during breakfast and I felt it on and off throughout the day. I was shocked and frightened by all of the injustice, selfishness, and willful manipulation going on all around me. But I was even more shocked and frightened at my response. I wanted to scream and kick every time I saw someone being treated unjustly or insensitively.
>
> That evening I had a meeting with the head of our pastoral ministry team. We were discussing the way various factions in the parish were trying to assert themselves to get their way. I was telling him that I observed that some of the teachers and families were trying to curry his favor. I suddenly became very aware that although he was smiling at me, he wasn't even listening. I got so damn mad! I wanted to scream at his indifference.
>
> That night, before retiring, I found myself praying silently, but in an angry voice. Suddenly it struck me that I had been looking at others, but also seeing myself. It was embarrassing. Funny thing, though, I found myself crying in relief. I am not normally an angry person. In fact, I go out of my way to avoid being angry. But in my tears, I kept hearing myself say, "No more Sister nice guy!"

A proclamation of meaning

In religious community an experience such as this one typically remains hidden behind sealed lips and a tight smile. It is not nice to be angry. Whether expressed overtly or in fantasy or merely in the privacy of our hearts, to experience anger is to feel guilt. Guilt is a reminder that we have violated the code of kindness.

The code of kindness instructs us to play the game of denial. This code instructs us to place being nice above being angry. When niceness is put in service of denial, it is inauthentic. To live by the code of kindness is to jeopardize the world of relationship; our capacity for authentic intimacy with self, other, the holy is more and more diminished as we grow habituated to a pseudo-intimate style of relating.

The code of kindness can be broken. In the above example, the person revealed a desire to stop being seduced by the code of kindness. For the woman in our example, this experience was the beginning of her return to authenticity. Other instances of negativity followed, and she suffered many months where relationships with self, other, the holy were accented by anger. However, her angry feelings were a vehicle for promoting the realization that she was living a spiritless existence. She had not been living her life; life had been living her!

It may happen that one day we will undergo a moment of awakening to the void within. We may realize one day that our lives consist of habits—of rising, being with others, working, praying—and we may become frighteningly aware that all these habits are lifeless, that they have no meaning or value in the context of our present life. We may become lonely, depressed, or anxious, or we may experience ourselves as empty or bored, or we may find ourselves angry. We may awaken to find ourselves drowning in a sea of nice smiles and empty words. We, too, may wish to lash out at others, or we may berate ourselves for having sold out to the inauthentic and the false.

If our angry feelings are in the context of nothingness, it is not uncommon for us to be thrown into the attitude of totalization. In such an attitude, each instance of injustice, insensitivity, or any negative moment we observe will represent the whole of life. Our lives will be experienced as the sum total of each negative act. Our whole being will get caught up in absurdity and meaninglessness.

If our anger is in the context of nothingness, the present will spread before us like an empty desert. The places, people, or situations where we are attempting to live lives of commitment will seem empty, dry, dead. The present will no longer be seen as a meaningful road to tomorrow, and to begin anew will seem impossible.

Creative response to a meaningless life

There are several possible ways of relating to such an experience. We may take flight. In our angry mood, we may give in to the frustrations we experience and cast off life form or life project. We may search for someone who is alive. We may look for new ways of life, ones that will provide as much distance as possible from the situations that our angry mood reveals as so unjust, insensitive, meaningless. Or we may withdraw into ourselves, closing ourselves off from the pain caused by a world we perceive as hostile.

Whether we are being treated unjustly or being unjust, the mechanisms of defense can assist us to gain the distance needed to calm down and see with more clarity. If, however, our angry mood is in the context of nothingness, invoking the mechanisms of defense or changing the situation will only provide momentary relief from pain. Nothingness will return, usually when it is least expected.

The call to authenticity with others

A change in self or situation may, however, be necessary. In the example used above, the experience of anger helped the individual to become more aware of the need to change herself. Adrian van Kaam instructs that change is only possible through the transforming power of love.[11] The niceness syndrome can be a counterfeit love, affecting our relational life—that is, our relationship to self, other, and the sacred.

While love may also include being nice, niceness and love are not identical. When we are being authentically nice or kind, our behavior is inclined to be well-disposed, benevolent. But it can also be a mask that hides indifference. Niceness can be expedient but not loving. Niceness may be a seduction to others, intended to make us popular, while also shielding us from the responsibility of witnessing to injustice in self or other, usually both.

Inauthentic niceness can be a way of promoting adulation and avoiding the self-awareness that can be revealed in an angry vision of reality. Inauthentic niceness can prevent us from seeing beyond the meaningless routine that may have dulled our sense of justice. Our niceness may also reflect self-concern; it may be a way of gaining power through manipulation and thus obscure the fact that our lives lack the vitality that can only be drawn from authentic love.

Inauthentic niceness can be condescending, as for instance when the "mentally healthy" minister to the "mentally ill," or when the "educated" minister to the "ignorant," or when the "saints" minister to the "sinners." This kind of niceness breeds resentment, for the recipients have been cut down, degraded.

Authentic love, however, offers the possibility of not being nice, as, for instance, when we point out to those we love a behavior or attitude that may be insensitive, selfish, or unjust. Such harsh moments of encounter are unsettling and disturb the inevitable complacence that settles over relationships when we have unwittingly drifted into the stance of pseudo-intimacy.

Quiet withdrawal into self for the purpose of allowing our negative experience to speak may enable us to risk the pursuit of deeper values, to risk living from our creative source, and to emerge into more authentic ways of being with others.

The void within

The voice of nothingness, revealing itself to us through the experience of anger, may make us painfully aware that although we profess a belief in prayer, our apostolate, love of neighbor, or a disciplined life, something is still missing.

In the angry cynical vision revealed in our example, the woman eventually discovered she had lost her belief in the transforming power of authentic, loving witness. She had given herself over to what St. John of the Cross might call the "herd," what we refer to as the code of kindness.[12] Fidelity to the angry voice within her eventually promoted the realization that she was hearing the voice of nothingness. She had drifted out of tune with life, with herself, with others, and with the holy.

In negative experience, she was thrown back upon herself. She discovered she had drifted into the pseudo-intimate stance of "Sister nice guy" and was bogged down. The graced call of authentic being whispered to her through the voice of angry cynicism. In this instance the woman religious was able to open herself to the grace of negative experience. If, however, she had been insulated from negative experience, she might not have realized the potential for growth inherent in such moments.

The woman in our example was facing the disappointment of her own emptiness. We observed earlier that it is not uncommon for people in that situation to be thrown into an attitude of totalizing. The acts of injustice she observed revealed to her that she was seeing nothing positive or redeeming within herself; thus, she could find nothing of value within others. In her angry mood, she witnessed to her own impotence to promote change. Her angry feelings revealed her belief that she was incapable of accomplishing anything. She felt she had done nothing, could do nothing, was nothing. Adrian van Kaam refers to this as the belief in pride-form—this belief fostered in part by our culture which instructs us to be self-sufficient.[13]

In the German culture people are viewed as inhabiting several worlds of relationship simultaneously. We inhabit an *eigenwelt* (personal world), an *umwelt* (a biological world, the world of senses), and a *mitwelt* (a world with others). When we lapse into the belief of self-sufficiency, we drift into the solipsism of the *eigenwelt;* the *mitwelt,* the social world, suffers a loss of vitality.

In our example the woman had drifted into the isolation of her personal concerns at the expense of the social world. Her presence to others in the social world had lost its vitality. She was fortunate; she was able to be awakened to a new, authentic, and more vital presence. She was indeed no more "Sister nice guy" (although it took many months for this full realization to be achieved). She was able to see the creative potential of negative experience. Over the next several months, people found her frequently angry and hard to endure, but they also experienced her as more genuine, authentic, and loving (although not so "nice" as previously!).

Others are not so fortunate. Some people respond pathologically by immersing themselves in anger, denial, self-pity, or fault-finding. They see others, the world, at fault. In the extreme, such people may view suicide as the only avenue of relief. Suicide is an act of personal despair, but it can also be the ultimate revenge, the ultimate angry response to a world perceived as unjust, insensitive, or hostile. In less severe pathology, persons may simply withdraw into negativity, isolating themselves, wallowing in the masochistic enjoyment of self-pity. In either case, the man or woman lives from the belief that others are at fault.

The need for others on the journey

Few of us ever get pathologically "stuck" in the severe sense. But we do undergo the ordinary spiritual pathology of the pride-form instructing us to journey alone. The pride-form instructs us that we can be self-sufficient persons who can provide our own fulfillment and be our own salvation. To inhabit the pride-form, according to van Kaam, is to take up a counterfeit form of life.[14] As an aspect of the functional self it tends to dominate life. Because the functional self is isolated in its possessing, grasping, and manipulating, it will not include in its management of daily life the form-giving message of the vital-self (*mitwelt,* the self of feeling and emotions), nor can it acknowledge its spirit- or relational-self (*mitwelt*). Thus, the functional self is not able to refrain from self-deception or from drifting into complacence. It has the capability to become isolated, to cut itself off from the deeper transforming power of reflection, appreciation, generosity, and acceptance.

In our interpersonal life Yahweh's voice may be delivered as a voice from an authentic other, or an authentic voice from within— both of whom are in truth the Ultimate Other. When we are open to negative experience from within self or from others, Yahweh's voice may become audible. We may hear it as an aggressive voice of love calling us to surrender the stance of inauthentic niceness and take up the stance of authenticity. In our despair we may hear a voice calling through the darkness demanding in love that we surrender the functional self along with our desperate desire to be accepted.

In our example, the sister heard the angry voice of nothingness calling from within. She was frightened, but was eventually able to arrive at a place where she could hear with a sense of humor. We are reminded of Meister Eckhart's formulation of spirituality: when the soul laughs at God and God laughs back, the Trinity is born.[15]

Witnessing to the sacred

We have been describing nothingness as revealed through the experience of anger. While we may not have had the experience of ordinary anger, the human condition (being-in-the-world-with-others) does create the possibility of being angry. Thus, since we are called into the journey of living spiritually through the human situation, it is possible we will need to discern the beckoning call of the Spirit in negative as well as positive experiences.

We have already noted that in being closed to the voice of nothingness, we can get blocked in relation to self and in relation to others. Though our life-form may be a witness to our belief in the value of prayer and reflection, we may get bogged down. At certain times in our lives we attempt to pray but find ourselves experiencing confusion and self-doubt. We may question our faith and find ourselves unable to vitalize our prayer. During such times, the Lord may invite us to the self-confrontation of creative anger. In such moments we may be frightened, and begin to blame ourselves, asking where we have failed. Or we may wonder how we could have lost our way.

Prayer life can be approached in the same way we approach other avenues of life. We can distance ourselves and close up, or we can remain within and see that a prayer of faith is about to be born.

When nothingness speaks to us in prayer we may react in pride and bitterness or revert to a previous style in order to get back to where we were. During such an experience, it is not uncommon to undergo a loss of faith. Should that occur, we may experience a desire to lash out at the sacred for bringing us to this point of pain, then abandoning us in darkness. Or, frightened by our experience, we may retreat to a more comfortable mode of "sensible" (formal) prayer and be satisfied to look at the sacred from a distance. Yet, as we have seen in our reflection on "self" and "other" there is another way to approach this painful experience of prayer: we may react in silence, learning to be still.

If nothingness is being revealed through the experience of anger at the sacred, we can expect the same eddy currents of emotion found in other areas of our relational life (doubt, guilt, shame), and we will be plunged into darkness. However, this may be the time to learn to pray in darkness, without thought, inspiration, or consolation.

Within our nothingness we may hear an aggressive voice challenging us to change. We may experience our tables overturned, our shekels scattered. We may hear a voice challenging us to face injustice in self, other, or situation. We may be asked to give our concern for justice over to the One who possesses the only power for change.

If that commanding presence succeeds in breaking down the barrier of the false and inauthentic, we may awaken to the realization that an authentic witness for justice springs from the ground of union. St. John of the Cross reminds us that the ground of union is cultivated by a willingness to die to self. He would tell us we must be willing to give up our power to invoke justice in order to be led to the place wherein resides the source of all justice. He would guide us with the wise instruction that it may be necessary to cross the desert of our own impotence—for as long as it is willed.

We find this wisdom of St. John of the Cross as he writes:

> One dark night,
> Fired with love's urgent longings
> — Ah, the sheer grace! —
> I went out unseen,
> My house being now all stilled;

St. John knows that when we are called by the voice of nothingness, we will at some point respond like the angry bride in the Spiritual Canticle:

> . . . Why, since You wounded
> This heart, don't You heal it?
> And why, since You stole it from me,
> Do You leave it so,
> And fail to carry off what You have stolen?
>
> Extinguish these miseries,
> Since no one else can stamp them out;
> And may my eyes behold You,
> Because You are their light,
> And I would open them to You alone.
>
> Reveal Your presence,
> And may the vision of Your beauty be my death;
> For the sickness of love
> Is not cured
> Except by Your very presence and image.[16]

Conclusion

We need not be afraid of negative experience. It is part of being human, part of our emergent selfhood, part of our spirit journey, part of the precariousness of human existence. To try to escape or avoid negative experience, be it sadness, disappointment, or anger, is to falsify who and what we are. To be open to negative experience is to risk the possibility of a deeper, more meaningful life. To be open to nothingness revealed through anger is to transcend each level of authenticity; to avoid the nothingness revealed through anger is to avoid the search for final encounter with the One who is all just. To be open to the negative voice of creative anger is to be open to the possibility that we are but a limited witness to justice. To be open to the creative potential of negative experience, such as anger, is to hear the wisdom of St. John of the Cross:

> ...In order to arrive at that which [we] knowest not
> [We] must go by a way that [we] knowest not.
>
> In order to arrive at that which [we are] not,
> [We] must go through that which [we are] not....[17]

As with all human experience, in the anger of nothingness there is mystery waiting only for us to be open in order that it may be revealed.

Endnotes

1. Michael Novak, *The Experience of Nothingness* (New York: Harper and Row, 1970), pp. 68–72.

2. William Kraft, *A Psychology of Nothingness* (Philadelphia: Westminster Press, 1974).

3. Jean Wahl, *Philosophies of Existence,* trans. F.M. Lory (New York: Schocken Books, 1969).

4. William L. Kelly and Andrew Tallon, eds., *Readings in the Philosophy of Man* (New York: McGraw Hill, 1967).

5. Karl Jaspers, *Reason and Existenz* (New York: Noonday Press, 1955).

6. Carol Tavris, *Anger: The Misunderstood Emotion* (New York: Simon and Schuster, 1982), pp. 38–44.

7. Theodore Isaak Rubin, *The Angry Book* (New York: Collier, 1970).

8. Tavris, *Anger.*

9. Adrian van Kaam, *Fundamental Formation* (New York: Crossroads, 1983), pp. 57–67.

10. Robert Bolt, *A Man For All Seasons* (New York: Vintage Books, 1962), p. 94.

11. Adrian van Kaam, *The Mystery of Transforming Love* (Denville, N.J.: Dimension Press, 1982).

12. *The Collected Works of St. John of the Cross,* trans. Kieran Kavanaugh, O.C.D., and Otilio Rodriguez, O.C.D. (Washington, D.C.: Institute of Carmelite Studies, 1964), p. 714.

13. Van Kaam, *Fundamental Formation,* pp. 266–267, 271–272.

14. Van Kaam, *Fundamental Formation,* p. 305.

15. *Meister Eckhart,* Franz Pfeiffer, ed., C. de B. Evans, trans. (London: John M. Watkins, 1947), p. 59. See also John Dunne, *The Reasons of the Heart* (New York: Macmillan, 1978), p. 48.

16. St. John of the Cross, *Collected Works,* p. 41.

17. St. John of the Cross, *Ascent of Mount Carmel* (Garden City, N.J.: Doubleday, 1958), p. 72.

Life-giving steam

Marie Hofer

Invitation • Response

Marie Hofer, Ph.D., is a full-time psychotherapist at the House of Affirmation in Montara, California. She studied at the Arnold T. Janssen College in Holland, received her master's degree at the De La Salle Graduate School in the Philippines, and her doctorate at the California School of Professional Psychology in San Francisco. From 1969 to 1972 Dr. Hofer established and coordinated the counseling and guidance services at Fu Jen Catholic University in Taiwan. She has taught languages in Italy and California. In 1979 Dr. Hofer joined the staff of the House of Affirmation; as a clinical psychologist she has a small private practice in San Francisco.

Invitation

I belong to the family named "Emotion." There are many of us: joy, fear, awe, grief, lust, courage, disgust, and of course myself, anger. Each of us can be productive if you treat us the right way. But each of us can also be quite temperamental. Like children we need guidance and direction. Many of you are afraid of us and prefer to separate us into good and bad categories. But let me remind you: we are all there for your good, to assure your survival and growth. What would life be without us? A child who does not smile, a body without color and tone.

We, the emotions, are biological; we live in your cells. While your mind may offer you labels and categories for us, it is your body that truly knows us. Take a moment right now and check yourself. What is your body sensing? What is your predominant feeling right now? Are you happy, sad, anxious, depressed, joyous, peaceful, or even angry? Whatever you are feeling is very good. Accept the feeling and exaggerate it a little bit, like blowing more air into a balloon. Now release the feeling slowly and relax. Being relaxed will help you to listen to me, for I have much to say about myself.

First, let me thank you for finally paying me some attention. Second, let me tell you that I have been mad at you for a long time because you have neglected, misunderstood, and shunned me. You would rather see me as hurt, stress, upset, fear, and guilt than what I really am—steam to keep your life engine going! Have you ever seen a dead face come alive for the first time when I was allowed on the scene? If my steam is channelled well, I move you; if not, I drive you crazy.

Why do you have so much trouble accepting me into your life when I am God's great gift to you? I must admit I am not exactly easygoing by nature. I am lively, forceful, and temperamental. I like to point out injustices, dangers, neglects, and hurts. I help you protect and mobilize yourself. I am unrelenting and convinced of my purpose. I will not be silenced.

Now I do not like to slam doors, kick, scream, and use other thunderbolt-and-lightning techniques. Only if I have been twisted and thwarted will I call attention to myself in such out-of-control manners. The biggest problem for me is lack of recognition. When you pretend I am not there I hide and pretend also. I become your neck pain, migraine, insomnia, ulcers, or cancer. Do you know that I can kill you?

Believe me, I would never do such nasty things except in self-defense. My nature is to serve you, help you clear the air, get things done, and feel free. Let me tell you the story of Hanna, an example of how I can work for or against you.

Hanna was born angry. Birth was an ordeal for both her and her mother. She was pulled into the world with forceps and upon arrival she nearly screamed her lungs out. Hanna knew without knowing that she was not wanted.

Things would have been better for her if she had been a boy. Four girls in a row was disappointing for her parents. Hanna loudly manifested her anger at the sensed rejection, keeping her frustrated parents busy during the day, and wide awake at night. "A colicky baby," their neighbors counselled, "just leave her alone until she cries herself to sleep." It worked. After a few horrendous nights, Hanna calmed down to more normal sleeping patterns.

Neglect, however, was not what Hanna had been screaming for. So she turned to other ways of showing her unhappiness. She became a fussy eater and threw up a lot. Mother hid her annoyance with this sickly daughter, as she had hidden her resentment about Hanna's birth. Moved by guilt to protect this child, her mothering turned to smothering. Father, a strict but caring man, was helpless with this scrawny youngster; he stayed away from her. The siblings went out on their own while Hanna attached herself to mother's apron strings. Her angry little heart found some comfort in being a quiet nuisance around the house. She had learned well to gain approval by conforming, and attention by being helpless and dependent. The neighbors saw her grow into a good little girl, shy and well-behaved.

Hanna was no longer angry, was she? Since she was now in school, her parents planned a five-day trip away from home. The first night with grandmother, Hanna seemed quite frightened and had trouble catching her breath. The condition worsened until she was painfully gasping and wheezing. She was rushed to the hospital and treated for an acute asthma attack. Alarmed, her parents cut short their trip. Finding Hanna lying pale and tired in a hospital bed was more than their guilty hearts could take. They cried and took her in their arms, assuring her that they would never leave her again.

So Hanna grew up well-protected from without but ill-adjusted from within. Her parents kept their promise, but when stress got bad at school, or later at work, Hanna suffered more asthma attacks. Things became very fierce for her when a young man began to pursue her. He asked for her hand, but Hanna declined on account of her illness. She lived a sheltered, fairly comfortable life with her parents, overshadowed only by her respiratory troubles. When her mother died, Hanna responded with a terrible asthma attack. Soon after, at age twenty-eight, she sought psychological help.

Since then she has learned a great deal about herself. She has come to understand how her resentment, anger, and rage had blocked her life-giving breath; how the asthma attacks were painful and ineffective attempts to release pent-up feelings. Instead of experiencing relief she had become more caught up in dependency and fear of separation. It was a struggle for her to release her fear and anger in more direct, constructive ways. She took up jogging, aerobics, and beating pillows. Hanna is beginning to flow with her feelings, to breathe normally, even joyfully at times. Six months have passed now without an asthmatic flare-up. Quite a record for her! She celebrated this event by writing a poem.

Ode to Asthma: Bondage and Birth

How I fear you, how I need you
breath of death to bring me life.

Gasping, wheezing, problems breathing,
terror stricken, attack! attack!

Throat all tangled, body mangled,
labor pains, I lose my mind!

Angry breathing, my releasing
mother hate so well disguised?

Crying, yelling is dispelling
fear of love and fear of life.

No more moaning, no more groaning,
separated—free at last!

How relaxing without taxing,
breathing in and breathing out.

Hanna and I, anger, have stopped the tortuous game. Now it is almost fun living together. Of course we still go at each other once in a while, and have to work through vestiges of our painful past. But generally she now recognizes and acknowledges my appearance, and she uses me quite well to keep her engine going!

As you can see, I need your cooperation in bringing life to you. There is a growing fear in me that you and I may already be too far apart. Just think of all the social ills, the feuds, injustices, rapes, and killings! How will we ever straighten out the mess? The task seems monumental.

Recently, I, anger, had a nightmare. I saw myself as a tiny life-containing seed. As I began to sprout and show my nature on the surface, I was disliked and ill-received. Attempts to hide me, bend me, even kill me, were unrelenting. However, my spirit was determined to live rather than to die; instead of being weakened by the attacks, I was strengthened. My roots and branches grew fiercely, taking on immense proportions. People looked funny, even stupid, as they walked around, most of them ignoring my evergrowing presence. Their pretense somehow served to add momentum, and feeding on myself, I began to envelop people, places, nations.

I awoke terror-stricken. "What is the message, God?" I prayed. "Am I behind the nuclear craze as well? Please help these humans to take charge of me." And lying there panicked, raging, praying, I knew I had another chance with you.

Response

To meet this challenge to grow up we must begin with ourselves. We have a history with our anger, as with all our emotions. There may be unfinished business regarding these emotions that hampers our efforts to move forward.

Anger was obviously present at birth when, shocked by the harsh reality of life, we angrily kicked and cried. This jolting experience started us breathing. How is your breathing right now? Shallow? Deep? Breathe deeply right now and relax.

Anger was also present in the "no" of our "terrible twos," and all the way up to adolescence, helping us proclaim our separateness to the world. I hope the world accepted our young protestations. If not, these tantrums may still be present in our stiff muscles and joints.

Let us do a quick body check right now. Which of your body parts are stiff or relaxed? How about standing up and throwing a mini tantrum? Just in case you have forgotten how it works: stamp one foot and then the other. Throw up your arms, waving and gesturing. Now add some noise, too. You can have fun doing this. It is also a great way of exercising and releasing tension!

And then anger was, of course, present in our emotional response to many situations which just did not feel right: a sibling's arrival that made us number two; a roughneck giving us a bloody nose for no reason. And how destructive it was to be told we should not be angry!

We also had good ideas crammed down our throats; we had to please and comply to buy acceptance; we were told to achieve but not to feel. Teachers were all too human at times, causing us to feel small, incompetent, embarrassed. Then there were the many bumps on the road of life.

It is important that we work through these experiences and create some distance. Begin to remember right now a situation that you did not like. Let the scene arise before you in as much detail as possible. What feelings are you reminded of? What feelings may you not want to feel? The choice is yours. Seeing old situations on a screen, as it were, is a great way of distancing ourselves from them. Now how about reversing roles and letting yourself see the scene from the other person's point of view? We are capable of being both the victim and the aggressor.

You may have to do these or similar healing exercises more than once. If strong emotions arise you may want to write them down, draw them, and/or share them with someone else. Releasing feelings from our hurtful past frees us to live more fully in the present moment.

To conclude, let us deal with a practical situation which would involve anger as a normal response. A friend, Gene, has not returned a valued book of yours which you need to teach a class tomorrow. Gene promised to deliver the book right after breakfast, but neither he nor the book has arrived. You will be without needed charts, which throws off your lesson plan.

We all know ineffective ways of handling this situation. "The bastard," you shout, "this is too much! I never want to see his face again!" You shake your fist, kick the dog, curse every soul on your way to school. Bang! goes the classroom door. The frightened students know that something minor has happened which they will pay for in a major way. Sure enough, there is the math test!

Obviously such reactions are far out of proportion to the situation. Are you using anger to conceal other feelings? How about disappointment, fear, loneliness? What about sexuality?

On the other hand, you may be too nice about the situation. "Gene is such a busy man," you say, "too much on his mind these days. Never mind those charts. I will just try to do something else, prepare another lecture. Why not?" Depression grows, masking the angry feelings pretty well except for your general irritability and an occasional mini explosion. "What is wrong?" ask your concerned friends. "Oh, it's just stress. Vacation will be coming soon."

Well, how about another response? "Hey, Gene, where is that book?" Your voice on the telephone carries annoyance. "I am so mad at you! I want that book right now! I don't care how you get it here. Hijack a helicopter if you have to!" But what if Gene cannot be reached? Well, you can kick a few pillows, or run a mile or two, imagining Gene under your feet. Or if you have no time simply acknowledge your anger and the need to deal with it later. Then why not tell your students the story of the missing book and the angry breakfast you had because of it. Involve them in your process and the responsibility for structuring the class. It could be the best lesson you have ever taught them: how to live constructively with anger.

In conclusion, let us thank God for anger. And thank you, anger, for being our life-giving steam.

Soured and sullen:
The indirect expression of anger

G. Martin Keller

Anger: What and when • Anger: An interpersonal emotion •
Anger: A social corrective • Two kinds of anger • Anger: A passion •
Expressing anger • The passive-aggressive personality •
The development of passive-aggressive behavior •
The passive-aggressive in religious communities • The suspect
emotional life • Anger as sin • Healthy ways of expressing anger

G. Martin Keller, O.S.A., Psy.D., is a full-time staff psychotherapist at the House of Affirmation in Whitinsville, Massachusetts. He received a master's degree in theology from Augustinian College, Washington, D.C., and a doctoral degree in psychology from Nova University in Florida. Before joining the staff of the House of Affirmation, Father Keller was involved in campus ministry and professor of pastoral studies at the Institute for Ministries at Loyola University, New Orleans, Louisiana. He is a member of the American Psychological Association, and a frequent lecturer and workshop facilitator.

In this presentation on anger I will begin by considering what anger is, why it happens, and how people handle it. My main emphasis will focus on the type of person who expresses anger in an indirect manner, the passive-aggressive or negativistic personality. I will then examine some possible reasons why such personalities gravitate toward religious communities. Finally, I will offer practical ways to manage anger in a healthy and beneficial manner.

Anger: What and when

Anger can be defined in a number of ways depending upon the elements emphasized. I want to discuss the function anger performs for us interpersonally and socially. Accordingly, I would define anger as an emotion that helps to regulate interpersonal relations through the threat of retaliation for perceived wrongs. I would also interpret anger as a passion rather than an action.

Anger occurs when a person perceives that he or she has been wronged, possibly by a harmful or potentially harmful action seen as unjustified. For example: your provincial has told you that you are up for reassignment to some other work in the college, and that she will consult with you at the proper time. Later that month you read in the community newsletter that you have been reassigned to teach third grade at Our Mother of Perpetual Sorrows. You perceive that you have been wronged unjustifiably. You are angry.

Or, you come upon a good friend being berated once again by a rather forceful co-religious—and once again your friend just stands there taking it, not standing up for himself. You perceive that he is hurting himself by his non-assertiveness, and you become angry at him.

If an action is not deliberate but easily avoidable, it might also be an occasion for anger. For example: Father Angelicus promises to have the car back in time for you to use it to pick up a close friend at the airport. At the proper time you look out into the parking lot and the car is there. But Father Angelicus is nowhere to be found—nor are the keys; they are in his pocket. In your opinion, although he sincerely forgot to put the keys back on the hook, the incident could easily have been avoided with sufficient care and forethought. You become angry.

To sum up then, anger is instigated by two general situations. In the first, someone deliberately and unjustifiably wrongs you, self, or an innocent third party. In the second, you are wronged in a way that is not deliberate, but could have been avoided.

Anger: An interpersonal emotion

Anger is occasioned by our interactions with other people. Now if we stub our toe on a table leg, we do not make the table stand in the corner for an hour. When we pass by the offending table later in the afternoon we do not insult it, or pointedly ignore it. Oh, we may yell or curse or even kick the table at the time, but later we feel a bit foolish about our behavior. These reactions are more a result of surprise, physical pain or frustration rather than of true anger. When we are really angry we direct that anger at another person or persons, or at institutions which can be symbolic of persons.

Specifically, at whom do we get angry? While it is true that we can get angry at anyone, it is more frequently a loved one or friend, or at least a well-liked acquaintance. We might get angry at someone who cuts us out of a parking space, and remember the incident later in the day. But imagine how much more intense our anger would be if the person who did this were a close friend.

Anger: A social corrective

Anger may be considered an interpersonal emotion in another sense as well. Not only do individuals become angry at other individuals, but socially anger serves to uphold accepted standards of conduct. The general social directive is that ordinarily people should not be angry. However, under certain conditions, reasonable men and women cannot help but become angry. If such persons respond in accordance with socially acceptable norms, then they are not held responsible for their feelings.

A typical condition under which reasonable people become angry is a violation of social norms, for example, a breech of etiquette, a broken promise, or the violation of some widely shared standard of conduct observed among friends—a violation which is seen as unwarranted and unjustified or avoidable. Anger then functions as a corrective, encouraging violators to conform in the future to socially accepted standards of conduct.

This does not mean that when you get angry at your best friend for having concealed the fact that he is going into the hospital for a serious operation, that you are doing your bit to uphold the social order. But it does mean that if you communicate your anger to your friend he will know that in the future he is to act in accordance with the widely accepted code of conduct for friends—that they share important life events with each other. Anger helps to regulate your interpersonal relationship with him.

On a somewhat larger scale, if you communicate your anger to the bursar of your community when you discover that the cook is being paid below minimum wage because she is slightly retarded and does not realize her rights, your anger functions as a possible corrective to this social injustice.

Two kinds of anger

We might also examine the motives of anger—or put in a different way—what people hope to accomplish by their anger. In this regard, two basic kinds of anger may be distinguished: malevolent anger and constructive anger. Malevolent anger is used to indicate dislike and to break off a relationship. Expressions such as "to get even" or "to get revenge" characterize this type of anger. Constructive anger, however, aims at strengthening a relationship, improving our image, or bringing about a change in the target of our anger for his or her own good. Constructive anger is the more frequent of the two. This is not surprising since friends and loved ones are most often the targets of our anger.

Anger: A passion

My last point in this general description is that anger might be considered a "passion." By that term I mean more than an intense emotion. I am considering the word "passion" in its etymological and literal sense: something that we suffer rather than something that we deliberately initiate. And this is generally true of all our emotions. We have ways of speaking about emotions that indicate that they are indeed passions or psychic events that happen to us or befall us: we are "caught up in happiness," and "laid low by sadness," "gripped by fear," "torn apart by envy or jealousy," or "carried away by anger."

Emotions are not premeditated actions. We do not say, "Well, I'd better plan my emotions for today. Let's see now, I've been feeling a bit depressed lately, so I could use a little happiness—maybe between 10:00 and 11:00 this morning. I could also do with a little more hope. I might be able to squeeze that in between 2:00 and 2:30 this afternoon." Rather, emotions befall us. It follows then that although we may be responsible for how we express our emotions, we are not generally responsible for experiencing them. Lust, jealousy, anger, sadness are not emotions we would choose to experience. And the point is that we do not choose them—we "suffer" them.

We have also heard the expression "crime of passion." This euphemism usually refers to some unlawful act committed while a person was under the immediate influence of an emotion so powerful that it diminished that person's capacity for rational thought and activity. The typical crime of passion involves an act committed under the influence of rage, anger, or sudden resentment. If a crime of passion is verified in a court of law, judges and juries tend to call for and pass more lenient sentences than for similar crimes committed with forethought or premeditation. Here there is a common under-standing and acknowledgement that the guilty parties were in some way not completely responsible for their actions since they were "swept away by their emotions."

Expressing anger

There are basically two ways in which people can express their anger—directly or indirectly. Those who express their anger directly tell the offending party clearly, with varying intensity and appropri-ateness, that they are indeed angry. They leave no room for doubt.

The indirect expression of anger, on the contrary, is neither clear nor straightforward. Oftentimes angry persons will not admit to themselves that they are angry. Sometimes the target of an indirect expression of anger is unaware that the offended party is angry. Many times the target of the anger is aware on some level that the person seems angry, but does not have a clue as to the reason.

There are myriad ways in which indirect anger may leak out of a person. It may be seen in one's use of humor—not a ha-ha sort of humor, but a biting and hurting type. What might be said with a smile, and received with laughter, will not leave people feeling good and light-hearted.

Cynicism and sarcasm are also indirect expressions of anger. People may laugh at the incongruity of what is being said if it is expressed skillfully, but upon further reflection they will see that it is in reality no laughing matter.

Anger may also be displaced onto someone else. The priest who is angry with his pastor or his associate may take it out on the altarboys or his students, and back in the rectory act in a rather distant and detached manner toward the offending confrere.

Why do we act this way? Why don't we express our anger directly and get it over with? One very compelling reason is that some of us do not realize that we are in fact angry. We cannot name our anger as such. Instead we may see ourselves as hurt or sad.

Even if I am aware of my anger, there may be fears within me powerful enough to stifle any direct expression. I may fear losing

control. If I begin to show even a little of what I feel, I will get so
caught up in it that I will lose my cool, start shouting, and wind up
looking like a fool.

I may fear that the target of my anger will lose control. If I get
angry at him, he may become angry at me and we will end in a fight
which could come to blows.

Perhaps I fear that the relationship will be broken off. I need her
friendship and if I become angry with her, she will not like me any
more, and she will no longer be my friend.

I may fear that I will hurt the other person seriously. If I show my
anger, he will be hurt. And since I like him, I don't want him to feel
bad.

I may fear that the other person will retaliate at some future time,
or that she is too powerful. "Who am I that I can get angry at her?" In
effect, I am saying that I am a nobody because of my low self-esteem.

Such fears do not dissipate the anger. They merely prevent its
direct expression. Since the anger is still there it will leak out in
indirect ways.

The passive-aggressive personality

Thus far I have discussed covert or indirect expressions of anger.
But there is a type of personality that, in addition to indirectly
expressing anger, also becomes ineffective socially and occupation-
ally. Those who use this means to punish the persons with whom they
are angry are the passive-aggressive or negativistic personalities.

The essential feature of the passive-aggressive personality is a
resistance to demands for adequate performance in both occupational and social functioning. This resistance is expressed indirectly
rather than directly; it is expressed passively rather than actively,
through procrastination, stubbornness, dawdling, inefficiency, and
"forgetfulness." The consequence of this behavior is pervasive social
and/or occupational ineffectiveness, even when more assertive and
effective behavior is possible. The name of this personality style is
based on the assumption that such individuals are passively expressing inner aggressive feelings.

Following are some examples of passive-aggressive behavior.

Father is sent by his bishop to teach in a high school instead of to
another parish as he had requested. Offering no protest to the bishop,
Father goes into teaching. But he is frequently late for class, seems

unable to maintain discipline in the classroom, often misses department meetings because of schedule conflicts with outside appointments, and is always at least three days late with his quarterly marks. Demands by the principal and the bishop for adequate performance are not met. Father gains the deserved reputation of an ineffective teacher.

The Sister choir director has not been placed on the Parish Centenary Celebration Committee as she had wished. She cancels some choir practices because of a persistent cold. She also selects several beautiful but difficult motets for the celebration. The choir performs quite poorly on the day of the festivities and as a consequence, Sister is fired.

Not having been invited to a dinner for close friends given by the Silver Jubilarian, Father fails to hear his alarm wakening him from his afternoon nap. He misses the jubilee mass. His absence is noted by all, but especially by the Father Jubilarian.

In day-to-day living, passive-aggressive persons appear sour, sullen, complaining, and unaccommodating. If you do them a favor, they resent being obligated; if you fail to do them a favor, they feel slighted. If you praise them for some talent, they are embarrassed and uncomfortable for being singled out. If you do not, they feel unappreciated. If they are selected for a leadership position, they complain about the lack of support. If they are passed over, they become critical and unsupporting of the appointed administration.

Such persons complain about everything; nothing seems right. The air is too fresh. The sky is too blue. The sun is too bright. The grass is too green. The food is too bland one day, too highly spiced the next.

It is demoralizing to be around passive-aggressive persons. They seem to resent the presence of joy or happiness, having neither of these qualities themselves. They resent the freedom of others, not experiencing in themselves any inner freedom.

I heard of a monk who used to check the car sign-out book several times a day. In the evening he would complain how empty the monastery seemed during the day. He would also lament the unavailability of cars, even though he himself rarely left the grounds. The monk died. In this particular community there was a custom that a memorial card with a picture of the deceased was published for each member of the community. One of the monks hung his memorial card on the wall overlooking the car sign-out book. Father could then continue to do in death what he had enjoyed doing in life.

If you think passive-aggressive people are difficult to live with, you are correct. But what must it be like for such persons to live with themselves? For not only are they bitter and resentful, but they also feel hurt and unappreciated. Not infrequently they will also feel guilty and remorseful about the way they are treating others, and depressed at the way their life seems to be going.

The development of passive-aggressive behavior

How do such people get to be that way? One of the most popular theories holds that as children passive-aggressive personalities did not get their dependency needs gratified. Their parents did not fulfill sufficiently their affectional needs. Yet they could not complain to their parents or in any way demand such attention, for they viewed their parents as so powerful and threatening that they did not dare express themselves directly. Or they would not risk losing the little support they did get from their parents. They began to practice letting out their rage at their parents in indirect and self-punishing ways. They wet the bed until they were eight or nine years old; they did poorly in school or failed to get along with their playmates. This behavior was a way of punishing their parents. It was also a way to get attention from their parents, even though the attention was often negative. Unfortunately they set up for themselves a series and then a pattern of failure experiences, all of which led to a severe deficit in self-esteem.

If passive-aggressive persons enter religious life, they will still be searching for gratification of their dependency and affectional needs. They will look to peers and particularly to superiors to care for them. If angry at a superior over an assignment, the passive-aggressive person may say, "Well when I have my first heart attack, that will show her what a mistake she made." Or, "He'll be sorry when I have my next nervous breakdown." Unfortunately such persons have not learned either to express their needs directly to the appropriate persons or to express clearly their feelings of anger and frustration at not having their needs met.

It may happen that if you hear descriptions of such persons from those outside the community, you would not recognize them. Outsiders may describe them as pleasant, gracious, and delightful personalities. Such persons are "street angels, home devils." They are able to deal well with outsiders with whom they have superficial interpersonal contact. However, they cannot but show their real colors when they attempt to live a more intimate life with others in community.

The passive-aggressive in religious communities

When I refer to "religious communities" I mean not only canonically established communities of men or women, but also presbyterates, parish councils and committees, and the wider varieties of organized religious groupings. It is with this sense of religious community that I quote the following passage:

> Passive-aggressive persons are extremely difficult to deal with because conflict never surfaces and they are unwilling to cooperate. They manage to maintain a rather serene picture of themselves as well-controlled, proper, nonviolent human beings. But they are not the peaceful or loving personalities they pretend to be. When they are confronted with the disruptive nature of their style, they do not easily give it up. Often they remain remote and inaccessible to healthy relationships. If any relationship begins to build, the passive-aggressive person quietly withdraws, leaving hurt behind. Unfortunately, this personality is common in religious communities.[1]

It is my contention that there are certain distorted elements of religious life that encourage the maintenance of a passive-aggressive personality style. It is also my belief that, fortunately, these distorted elements are beginning to be recognized as such. As they are exposed, healthier ways of living in religious communities become available. But they have been with us a long while and no doubt will continue to influence to some extent the way we live in religious communities.[2]

The suspect emotional life

Many of us are aware, for example, of a spirituality which overemphasizes the rational faculties of men and women and casts undue suspicion upon our emotional life. The ideal proposed, it seems, would be the attainment of a mental attitude whereby we would no longer be bothered by desires of any kind.

I remember an incident from my novitiate in New York. One classmate complained to another that he never passed along anything

at the table. The novice, who was quite thin and ascetic-looking,
replied: "Ask for nothing; refuse nothing." This example ostensibly
deals with food and drink. But the underlying philosophy has been
applied to our emotions as well. We should ignore them or at least
keep them under the strict control of our intellect. The ideal would be
to feel nothing. Sexual feelings, anger and irritations, feelings of envy,
jealousy, and competition, to name a few, are seen as wrong and
needing to be dispelled. The distinction between feeling an emotion
and acting on that emotion has been totally ignored. This philosophy
encourages passive-aggressiveness insofar as it discourages the display or expression of anger and annoyance and seems to hold up rigid
control as an ideal.

   If one of the goals of religious living is to know ourselves, à la
St. Augustine's prayer, "Lord, may I know myself, may I know thee,"
then the reasonable thing is to pay attention to our emotions so that
we may come to an understanding of what they are saying to and
about us.

Anger as sin

   Another element disruptive of healthy living within religious
communities is the rigid view of anger as sin, another factor which
discourages the direct expression of angry feelings.

   There are also a number of overemphases in religious life which
discourage an assertive expression of anger.

Altruism

   While it is true that others are our brothers and sisters under the
common fatherhood and motherhood of God, we too are sons and
daughters of the same God. As such we have an inherent dignity
which is to be acknowledged not only by others, but also and certainly by ourselves. When we ignore our own rights and feelings and
believe that calling attention to our hurts and irritations is no more
than simple selfishness, we shut ourselves off from our basic dignity
and open ourselves to feelings of anger, guilt, and low self-esteem.

Perfectionism

   I would imagine that some have indeed reached the unitive and
illuminative ways. I suspect that many of us are still stuck in the

purgative way and that some of us are even pre-purgative from time to time. Perfection is what we are called to, the ideal toward which we strive. The tension between what we are and what we are called to is part of the stuff that makes up our spiritual journey. Expecting too much of ourselves or paying too much attention to the expectations of others will hinder us from understanding where we are on our journey. If anger is part of our current journey we would do better to deal with it than to bewail it.

Dependency

The capability of becoming overdependent on religious life also makes community living an ideal place for passive-aggressive persons. They have strong dependency needs to begin with, and they can continue to depend on the system to take care of them even if they fail to contribute effectively to the community by their work. When religious communities fail to emphasize accountability and to encourage personal responsibility, they also fail to help the passive-aggressive personality move toward healthier ways of living within community.

Healthy ways of expressing anger

It is said that good communication is good psychology. In fact, Virginia Satir, one of the pioneers of family therapy, holds that a healthy family is characterized by clear and direct communication. Dysfunctional families do not know how to communicate well. The same is true for functional and dysfunctional persons.[3]

In general, a good communicator is one who has the ability to use the first person pronoun "I," followed by an active verb, and ending with a direct object to praise, criticize, evaluate, or report emotional responses to another person in that person's presence. Specifically, if I own or take responsibility for my feelings, if I speak for myself, if I am concrete and specific, and if I express my true message, then I am communicating in a functional and healthy way.

Another helpful way to express one's anger directly is to be assertive in one's communication. Assertiveness is a form of interpersonal behavior in which one expresses one's thoughts, opinions, beliefs, or emotional states honestly, directly, and appropriately. Assertive behavior can be contrasted with non-assertive behavior which is dishonest, indirect, and inappropriate. It is also different from aggressive behavior which, although honest and direct, is inappropriate.[4]

When I use the word "appropriate" I mean more than making a good judgment call as to what is appropriate in a given circumstance. I also mean that the expression of anger is appropriate to what is being felt. For example, if I say, "I am angry with you for breaking your promise to support my resolution in the House Chapter," yet I speak in a gentle and calm voice with a radiant smile on my face, this attitude is not appropriate to the message I am giving. Where is the passion? You will remember I said earlier that anger is, as all emotions are, a passion. We experience it, we suffer it, we are carried away by it to a certain extent.

Not only will people not hold us totally responsible for a raised voice, flushed face, and clenched hands—they expect it. In fact, if we say that we are angry while speaking in a cold and calculating way, not showing any passion, people may suspect our motives. They may see us as more brooding and cunning and much more angry than we say we are. We may even be regarded as vengeful.

Finally, I offer two questions to ask ourselves as we wonder whether we would do well to express our anger.

"Is it worth it?" Sometimes it is just not worth it to express our anger. The stakes may be too high, and the odds are that it will do no good. It may even make the situation worse. This is particularly true if the target of our anger is a person who should not be held responsible for his or her actions, because of age or ignorance or infirmity. If I realize that the person cannot profit from the experience of being confronted with my anger (a senile patient, for example), I would do better to forget about it.

"Will I feel better or worse afterwards?" Gradually, we learn to know ourselves rather well. If I have come to see myself as a person who rarely expresses anger, but who goes around brooding, sad, resentful, then I would do well to learn how to become assertive and expressive of my anger in a clear and direct manner.

I would like to end on an encouraging note. A study by James R. Averill found that both the person who expressed anger as well as the person who was the target of the anger more frequently than not concluded that the expression of anger was a positive experience that benefited their relationship.[5]

Endnotes

1. R. Hammett and L. Sofield, *Inside Christian Community* (New York: LeJacq, 1981), p. 75.

2. D. Parsons and R. Wicks, eds., *Passive-Aggressiveness: Theory and Practice* (New York: Brunner/Mazel, 1983).

3. Virginia Satir, *Conjoint Family Therapy* (Palo Alto, Cal.: Science and Behavior Books, 1967).

4. A. Lange and P. Jakubowski, *Responsible Assertive Behavior* (Illinois: Research Press, 1976).

5. James R. Averill, *Anger and Aggression: An Essay on Emotion* (New York: Springer-Verlag, 1982).

Anger at God

Brendan P. Riordan

The rage we dare not name • What makes us angry at God? •
A historical perspective • What do we do with our anger
at God? • Healing our anger

*Reverend Brendan P. Riordan, M. Div., M.A., director of education for the
House of Affirmation, holds graduate degrees in psychology and theology.
Prior to joining the staff of the House of Affirmation, Father Riordan served
as a parish priest, seminary professor, and diocesan director of church
vocations. He is a certified alcoholism counselor, and has lectured widely in
the United States and abroad on psychotheological issues. Father Riordan is
spiritual advisor to the National Guild of Catholic Psychiatrists, and co-
author of* Desert Silence: A Book of Reflection on Methodology and Prayer.

The rage we dare not name

A few years ago, at Christmas time, I was visiting a hospital and
stopped in the pediatrics ward to say hello to the youngsters who
would be spending the holiday season there. To me, there is nothing
sadder than children confined to a hospital at Christmas. The pain of
illness is compounded by the fact that they will miss all of the
excitement and joy of the season.

I moved from bed to bed, room to room, asking the children
their names and saying a word or two to each of them. One little boy
caught my attention; there was something about the weariness in his
eyes, the near translucence of his skin, that made him stand out. I
went to his bed and spoke to him. He told me his name was Brendan,
and when I said that my name was Brendan, too, he was interested,
almost amused. He had never before met anyone else with his name,
and we began a pleasant and surprisingly "grown-up" conversation.
As he spoke, I began to take in his appearance in more detail. He was
very small, even for his five years. His thin hair was very blond, and
his eyes were a watery bluish color; his very pale skin was marked in
several places with terrible bruises.

He caught me looking at one particular mark on his arm and
said, "That's from the needles." I asked what the needles were for, and
he told me that he was getting blood transfusions. We talked for some

time, and after a while his mother arrived. When we had the opportunity, she and I left little Brendan's bedside and walked out to a
lounge. His mother explained to me that Brendan had leukemia, and
was not expected to live very much longer. Her face was lined with
exhaustion, and there was a sad bitterness in her voice. I asked if
she would mind if I came again to visit Brendan, and she said she
would appreciate that.

Over the next few weeks, I made many visits to little Brendan,
and I began to feel quite close to him and to his mother and father. At
one point, his parents told me that they regretted he would not be able
to receive First Holy Communion. We arranged that I give first
communion to Brendan in the hospital.

Brendan died very suddenly, much sooner than was expected,
and his parents' grief was overwhelming. A few days after the funeral,
his mother came to visit me at my rectory and asked me to come to the
church with her. We tried to pray together, but her tears made that
very difficult. She sat in the pew, hunched over and hugging herself,
sobbing softly. Finally, with a great effort, she got to her feet. I
thought she wanted to leave, and so I began to stand, too, but as I was
getting up, she raised her fist and shook it at the altar and began to
shout. Much of what she shouted was nothing more than incomprehensible groans that welled up from deep inside her, but among those
pained groans I made out the harsh words in which she was cursing
God. She cursed him for taking her little boy away; she cursed him for
allowing her to give birth in the first place; she cursed him for
allowing her to be born herself. In one breath she cursed God for
doing nothing to help her and her son, and in the next breath she
cursed God for doing too much, for intruding in her life with his
insensitivity.

In the end, she swooned, and I reached out to prevent her falling
over as she collapsed in a heap on the pew. All of the terrible rage that
had poured out of her exerted a calming and purifying effect, and in a
very few days she began to "let go," to give her child up to God with a
certain measure of peace of heart.

I think of that little boy and of his family often, and whenever I
do, I relive the horror I felt as that broken-hearted woman, crushed
and yet with a kind of dignified strength, stood so terribly alone and
spat out her rage at God. At that moment in her mind, God had
abandoned her, at best; at worst, he had purposely wounded her more

deeply than she had ever dreamed possible.

I remembered that mother's grief, and her ultimate peace of heart, years later when I read Harold S. Kushner's book, *When Bad Things Happen to Good People.*[1] Rabbi Kushner wrote that book because he had experienced the profound grief of losing his young son, Aaron, to a rare childhood disease. He began to write the day he heard the diagnosis of Aaron's condition, and from that day he visualized the dedication page: beneath his son's name would be the words King David spoke after his son's death, "'Absalom, my son! Would that I had died instead of you!" But about a year and a half after his son's death Kushner began to visualize the dedication in a different way. He saw the page bearing other words of King David, words he spoke after the death of an earlier child:

> When David saw the servants whispering, he said to them, "Is the child dead?" And they said, "He is dead." And David rose and washed and changed his clothing and asked that food be set before him, and he ate. The servants said to him, "What is this that you are doing? You fasted and wept for the child when he was alive, and now that he is dead, you get up and eat!" And David said: "While the child was yet alive, I fasted and wept, for I said, 'Who knows whether the Lord will be gracious to me and the child will live?' But now that he is dead, why should I fast? Can I bring him back again? I shall go to him; but he will not return to me" (II Samuel 12:19-23).

Once he envisioned this dedication, Kushner knew that it was time to write his book, not a book about self-pity, but a book about facing and accepting the tragedy that had befallen him and his family, a book affirming life.

Priests, religious, and lay people who minister in hospitals sometimes hear people expressing anger at God when a dearly-loved friend or relative dies. For the most part, however, the problem of anger at God is one we never discuss. We have been taught to repress and deny it, and there are very genuine guilt feelings associated with anything approaching anger at God; such feelings produce a sense of personal sin. A very powerful taboo surrounds the whole question of being angry at God, and our respect for that taboo has led us to neglect what I believe is an important subject.

Anger at God is a very real problem, and it occurs much more extensively than only in the cases of bitterly mourned deaths. Priests and women and men religious are, I believe, particularly inclined to feel this anger, and it manifests itself in a broad variety of ways. Minor physical ailments, substance abuse, depression, and passive-aggressive behavior, like constant lateness and appointments "forgotten" and missed, often have their roots, for ministerial persons, in a form of anger at God.

The most profound manifestation of anger at God I have seen was the tragedy of a woman religious I knew rather well. She had spent her whole life in service to the poor and the aged, and over the years she had become a very angry person. She was overwhelmed by the injustice and the suffering she observed every day, and enraged by it. She involved herself in every possible form of social protest, and she freely expressed her indignation in the face of greedy men and women who cared more for their own comfort and profit than for the sufferings of the poor and forgotten.

In the end, she turned from protests and expressed her profound anger at a God who, though supposedly all-powerful, permitted mortals to inflict such suffering on one another. In the end, she committed suicide, taking by her own hand the life God had given her. In that act of self-destruction she ritually declared her independence of God, asserting that she was not powerless in his presence. Yet, by ending her own life, she drained all power out of herself in the very act of declaring her radical independence.

In attitudes and acts far short of suicide, many of us cry out against what God has permitted to happen to our lives, our world, and our plans. Many older religious and priests are angry because the security they had looked for in their vocations has been taken away by changes in the Church. Many younger women religious are filled with rage because they perceive themselves as oppressed by a male-dominated Church, and by a male image of God.

Seminarians and young people in formation are frustrated and angry because they feel an emptiness at the center of their being, and because they seem to hear nothing from God in spite of their straining efforts to listen to him. Many of our friends of all ages have been faithful to celibacy, and now find themselves lonely and without emotional support.

Large numbers of women and men who have left active ministry are hurt, frustrated, and angry because they feel rejected by the Church to which they gave much of their lives. We who have remained often feel a good deal of anger at the Church and at God for allowing so many good and dedicated people to feel so abandoned. Numerous lay persons have left the Church feeling that they have been rejected by a Church which does not understand their lives or their problems, and by a God who is insensitive to their real-life sufferings.

What makes us angry at God?

St. Thomas Aquinas says that we can never really be angry at a person who is subordinate to us. He maintains that anger is always directed at persons who are, in one sense or another, our "superiors," with some kind of "power" over us. Our anger at such people is caused by the fact that they have somehow robbed us of our freedom and dignity by reminding us that we are powerless in their presence.

If we seem to be angry at a person in a subordinate position, then we have really "promoted" that person, making him or her superior to us by allowing ourselves to feel "powerless" in some way. Many instances of everyday anger are rooted in such processes. A manipulative child enrages its parent when it corners the parent into doing or putting off something. In such a case, by a combination of manipulation on the one hand, and abdication of authority on the other, the apparent "subordinate" has taken charge and reduced the "superior" to powerlessness.

One of the most touching and tragic forms of anger is that felt when a spouse dies. It is often an important part of the grieving process for the widowed spouse to admit anger and resentment against the husband or wife who has died, and to be reassured that those feelings are natural and normal. The root of this kind of anger is the feeling of being abandoned: "How could you leave me alone this way!" People who feel that they are mature and in charge of their own lives are suddenly and brutally reminded that they are powerless in the face of death.

There is a significant degree of selfishness at work in these feelings, and that selfishness is the source of much of the guilt feeling associated with anger at a dead spouse. The selfishness involved reaches back to the weakest part of the relationship before death. A person had felt somehow "in control" of the spouse, and the latter's death is the ultimate statement of independence. It reduces the widowed spouse to the ultimate position of powerlessness.

This tendency to see ourselves as the center of the universe, to interpret all events as either "gains" or "losses" in our own personal lives, is a remnant of a much earlier stage in our personal development, one that remains with most of us throughout our lives. Freud speaks of "infantile omnipotence," and describes it as the infant's impression that the whole world revolves around it. Jean Piaget has also offered a very careful analysis of the phenomenon.

Piaget is fascinated by the newborn child's exploration of its environment, especially by the infant's apparent attempts to identify the limits and extension of its own body. He points to the often-observed fact that infants are prone to reach out with their hands to take hold of their feet, and they seem pleased to spend hours staring at their own hands and feet, apparently awestruck at their ability to make these strange limbs move at will. Piaget maintains that the newborn does not distinguish itself from its environment. He holds that the infant's world is completely undifferentiated; the infant is not so much the "center" of the world, it *is* the world.

Slowly, by observing its own body and movements, the infant begins to make the necessary distinctions. It observes that some parts of the world—the parts of its own body—can be moved by an act of the will. Other parts of the world—the inanimate objects of the physical environment—cannot be moved at all, or else they move against the infant's will, crashing down and causing great commotion.

But there are other elements in the environment, rather ambiguous animate objects. Clearly these "things"—mother and father and certain other persons in the environment—are not part of the infant's body, but they are more amenable to its will than are inanimate objects. The infant can cause these "things" to move and to attend to its needs by calling out, by crying, by wetting, and so forth.

Healthy personal development implies that we will begin gradually to relinquish this manipulative hold over others, learn to communicate our needs, and accept our responsibilities. When a child loses a parent to death, he or she often experiences a tremendous rage. The child feels abandoned by the parent, and is angry because this person on whom so much depended has gone away. The remnants of "infantile omnipotence" are rudely destroyed as the child has its face rubbed in its own powerlessness: no amount of calling or manipulating can ever cause the deceased parent to respond again, and that sense of loneliness and impotence gives rise to profound and forbidden anger.[2]

The anger at God felt by many disillusioned priests and religious is very closely related to this anger directed at parents. In fact there is a symbiotic relationship between our anger at God and our anger at our parents: the one feeds the other. Our anger at God is often an expression of our unresolved feelings of anger toward our parents, and our manifestations of anger at our parents, who are "implicated with God" in the process of our being brought into being, are often surrogates for our inexpressible feelings of anger at God.[3]

In many cases, the anger and frustration of priests and religious are rooted in the destruction of their image of God. Changes in the Church, pressures of community living, or the demands of ministry often force us to put away our old notion of God's identity and begin searching for a new understanding of his being. When our "old God" "dies" in this way, we can find ourselves filled with feelings of rage and abandonment not unlike those experienced by children whose parents have died. Too little attention has been paid to the need to allow ourselves to grieve over the "death" of the God and the God-images of our childhood. We must learn to apply a grieving process like that of Elizabeth Kübler-Ross to help our sisters and brothers overcome the disappointment and disillusionment that often accompany the bitter process of "coming of age." Ours is a faith which demands that we be always ready to reform our image of the God who can never be captured by human imagination.

disappointment and disillusionment that often accompany the bitter process of "coming of age." Ours is a faith which demands that we be always ready to reform our image of the God who can never be captured by human imagination.

Father Herbert Smith, a member of the Jesuit community at St. Joseph's College in Philadelphia, has spoken of this trauma of discovering the "absence of God" in this way:

> We must try to find out why this discovery of the absence of God is a true discovery, and a necessary one, and what its meaning is. Why is it that the world made by God no longer reveals to the apostle the traces of God she used to find in its beauty and goodness? The psalmist too asks why: "Why, O Lord, do you hide from me your face?" (Ps. 88:15). The psalmist is not pleading to see the uncreated face of God, for he knows that was forbidden even to Moses in this life. No, he is trying to see God's "created face" in his works and his providence, and cannot, as he

makes clear: "You have taken my friends away" (88:9). The people and things which used to be his "friends" now only oppress him and tug at him and, as it were, shut God out.[4]

A mechanism similar to the one which operates when a child loses a parent is at work in the bereaved spouse. To the extent that the marital relationship had been marked by unresolved remnants of "infantile omnipotence," the widowed spouse will be angry at the deceased spouse. The death of a friend or relative is the final step by which one person moves beyond the reach of another, and it is the ultimate announcement of our own powerlessness over our environment.

The more intimately dependent we have been on another person, the deeper is our rage at that person's failure to respond to our needs—especially that absolute failure to respond which is death. At the same time, the more intimately dependent we have been on a particular person, the more powerful is the taboo against expressing our anger at that person's death.

All of this applies most precisely to our relationship with God. That relationship involves the most intimate dependence conceivable. We depend on God for our very existence, and God is the ultimate "superior" for all of us. Our absolute dependence on God makes us absolutely enraged at his unbounded freedom, at his absolute otherness, at our complete lack of control over him. When God fails to respond to our needs, when we sense that he has abandoned us or allowed evil things to happen to us, we are devastated. Our rage is nearly boundless, but an enormously powerful taboo prevents us from expressing our anger. If our wound is deep enough to cause us to overcome the taboo, we are left with complex feelings of guilt and personal sin. We would feel guilty enough if we expressed anger at a parent or spouse who abandoned us in death, but to express anger at God for failing to hear our prayers is unthinkable.

As our dependence and intimacy increase, so does our potential to be angry if we are left unsatisfied. At the same time, the taboo grows too, piling more and more guilt on us if we express our anger.

The same mechanism is at work in many other psychic areas. For example, the intimate language we use in prayer leads, surprisingly often, to the momentary arising of sexual images involving Jesus or Mary. When such images do flit across the imagination, the normal feelings of shame and guilt that would be associated with inappropriate sexual fantasies are magnified into sacrilege. Our profound and intimate dependence on these "ultimate superiors" gives rise to complex and powerful taboos. To express anger at God is as unthinkable as to entertain sexual fantasies about Jesus or Mary. But in either case, to repress these "unspeakable" feelings results in redirecting their energy inward, towards the self, a most destructive process.

A historical perspective

As Jean Piaget and other writers on the subject of child development point out, an essential element in personal growth is the process of "locating" oneself and properly identifying one's role in the world.

In the Middle Ages, the "age of faith," the vast community of the Church reached out to embrace all. Each person had a proper place in that great body, a proper set of relations with other Christians in the world, with the saints long dead, and with generations yet to be born. The human person was seen as the crowning glory of God's creation, and the human family, its history, and needs were the clear center of the cosmos. Since the Middle Ages there has been a gradual erosion of that certainty about our place in the universe, and a disintegration of that vast fabric of societal support.

In his somewhat dated, but still provocative book, *The Third Revolution*, the psychiatrist Karl Stern traces the three major steps in the process by which the myth of humankind's centrality has been dissolved.

Stern points out that Copernicus's theory of the heliocentric universe displaced the earth from the center of the cosmos; Marx's notion of the class struggle and other great historical forces which shape society removed the individual from the center of human society; and Freud's psychoanalytic revolution displaced the self and personal consciousness from the center of the universe.[5]

Although we may take these notions for granted, it is important that we understand the enormous trauma our race has experienced in learning to grasp and deal with them. Each of them poses a profound challenge to common sense. After all, any fool can see that the sun revolves around the earth; one need only look up at the heavens and follow the sun's course across the sky.

Copernicus upset not only our ancient cosmology, but also our epistemology, our theory of knowledge. He pointed out that our senses deceive us, and so we need something more than our senses in order to find the truth.

Step by step, each of these "revolutions" displaced us personally, and left us with profound questions: if we are not the standard by which all of reality must be judged and evaluated, what are we? If we are not at the center of the universe, where are we?

These fundamental issues are, in one sense, even more pressing for priests and religious than they are for others. In so many ways we depend on the Church and on our communities for our identity. This dependence, this "powerlessness," this clear and plain noncentrality puts us in the vanguard of those seeking to locate and identify themselves. The high emotional cost of this process is productive of rage and frustration.

A companion consideration is also productive of a great deal of anxiety: if we are not the center of the universe, who or what is the center? There is a growing suspicion in our modern age that there is no center to the universe at all, or that at the center of things there is nothing but chaos.

Our national experience here in the United States seems to bear out that suspicion. Until 1963, we were a very naive people. Until then, we generally believed that history's great moments had great men and women behind them, and that history's great tragedies had great causes behind them. We believed that it was the genius and the courage of people like Thomas Jefferson that had established our country, and that science's great progress was the result of the brilliant insights of great people like Isaac Newton and Madame Curie. On the other hand, we believed that great tragedies were the result of the coming together of great forces: Lincoln was assassinated as the last dramatic moment in the epic struggle of the War Between the States, and all of the suffering of the Second World War was the result of the superhuman evil of Nazism and its monstrous leader, Adolf Hitler.

But in 1963 our national self-confidence was shattered when our President was murdered by a single man whose motivation was completely unclear. Like most Americans, I remember vividly where I was when I first heard that President Kennedy had been shot. The first report I heard was the erroneous one that "they" had shot the

President, and that our Armed Forces had been put on alert to protect the country against what we feared was still to come.

When I learned that we were being asked to believe that this great tragedy was the work of a single insignificant man like Lee Harvey Oswald, my fear, sadness, and apprehension gave way to a new and deeper feeling of rage. If this were true, then there was no great cause behind this tragedy, and there never had been any way that we could have protected ourselves and our President from these events. A complex conspiracy could have moved us to action, but Oswald's meaningless act reduced us to absolute powerlessness.

Classical philosophers have called this fear that at the center of things there is nothing but unfeeling chaos the "Problem of Evil." Rabbi Kushner speaks of it as the problem of the "bad things that happen to good people." Theologians wrestle with the question, "How can a good and all-powerful God permit evil things to happen?" There seems to be no satisfactory answer, and we are left to fall back on the fact that earthquakes and hurricanes and assassins are free to do their work at random. This question of the Problem of Evil is the centerpiece of the Book of Job, which concludes that there is no answer to the question.

Long ago I was taught a problem-solving technique that has served me well over the years. If I am struggling with a question that seems unanswerable, it is sometimes useful to turn the inquiry around and ask whether the question itself has been stated clearly enough, whether the question I have posed is really the question that needs an answer.

The question posed by the Problem of Evil seems to be: "How can God permit. . .to happen?" In fact, the real point of the question is: "If *I* were God, *I* would never permit such a thing to happen!" Analyzing the question in this way results not so much in questioning God's power and the way he uses it, but rather in facing my own powerlessness and the anger I feel because of it. I am deeply angry at God because his system for running the universe brings me painfully face-to-face with my own powerlessness.

Toward the end of the Book of Job, God begins his address to Job and his friends this way:[6]

> Who is this obscuring my designs
>   with empty-headed words?

Brace yourself like a fighter:
>   now it is my turn to ask questions
>   and yours to inform me. (38:2-3)

God offers no explanation of his ways, no apology for his behavior. Rather, he shows that Job is asking the wrong questions, that he cannot possibly understand God's intentions or judge God's ways by human standards:

Where were you when I laid the earth's foundations?
When all the stars of the morning were singing with joy....
Who pent up the sea behind closed doors
>   when it leapt tumultuous out of the womb,
When I wrapped it in a robe of mist
>   and made black clouds its swaddling bands?
>>   (38:4-6, 8-9)

Our anger at God comes from our realization of our own powerlessness. It is our cry of rage at the fact that we are not God, and that God's ways are incomprehensible to us. In the long run, our anger at God is the modern version of idolatry, in that it is a cry of disappointment at our recognition that we are not all-powerful, that we cannot call God to judgment for his acts.

> All modern commentators agree that the particular forms of primitive idolatry have been outgrown. In the modern, secular, demythologized world, literal worship of finite objects is impossible. Yet while idolatry in its ancient sense is dead, something intrinsically related to it is very much alive. Nor am I referring to the slick, metaphorical context of "worshipping" wealth and/or sex—realitites which have been eagerly embraced by many, but which merely mimic the true meaning of the term. This new idolatry which now arouses God's jealousy has even infected religious life.
> On the most personal level, the phenomenon to which I refer might be called "internalized idolatry." It springs from an intoxication with our own finite insights. It possesses the mask-like deceptiveness of the ancient idols.[7]

What do we do with our anger at God?

It is normal and healthy, if not necessarily morally good, for anger to express itself in aggression. Let us return for a moment to the example of President Kennedy's assassination. If we had been convinced that the killing was part of a great conspiracy plotted by some foreign power, we could have directed our anger into some form of aggression: we could have ordered diplomats out of our country; we could have seized foreign property; we could have engaged in military action to punish the aggressors who had violated our security and killed our President. I do not suggest that any of these courses of action would have been right; I only mean that they would have been satisfying outlets for our anger.

The fact of the matter was that we had nowhere to channel our anger, no form of aggression that would have been satisfying. Even if Lee Harvey Oswald had not been killed and was available for punishment, to take even civilized aggressive action against him would have been unsatisfying. His insult to us was too profound, his act of reducing us to powerlessness was too complete, and there was nothing we could do to satisfy ourselves and purify the anger in our hearts.

Our anger at God has much the same quality. There is no satisfying and purifying form of aggression to balance what we perceive God has done or permitted to be done to us. In the first place, aggression against God is impossible; and, at any rate, it is unthinkable because of the powerful taboo that surrounds such a concept.

Psychologists maintain that aggression with nowhere to go is ultimately turned inward. This aggression against the self is manifested in the form of depression. I would like to suggest that the 1960s were an age of depression, a decade of rage with nowhere to go. I believe that our national psyche was depressed because our anger at meaningless assassinations, senseless wars, and unmanageable social problems was directed inward, and we began to hate ourselves. We hated our country, our military, our industries, our universities, and our churches. It was a time filled with a deep rage that had no proper target, and thus we became enraged at ourselves.

I believe that our anger at God is just such an insoluble anger: there is no "aggression" that would make us feel better or resolve that anger, and so it is directed inward, against ourselves. On the more superficial level, our anger at God makes us angry at ourselves because of the taboo against such feelings: we experience guilt and a sense of sin. On a much deeper level, we experience depression. Our psyche, to protect itself against the bad feelings of guilt and sinfulness, represses the feeling of anger. The product of that repression is aggression against the self, or depression.

I am making no original contribution to the treasury of psychoanalytic scholarship if I say that I believe depression is the chief characteristic of troubled priests and religious in today's world. I have seen it in my own daily work with my troubled colleagues and it has been the common experience of those who provide therapeutic services for persons in ministry. As a group we are people filled with rage that has nowhere to go; we are filled with aggression which is directed inwards and produces depression; we demonstrate complex patterns of passive-aggressive behavior.

Most persons with psychological training have heard of "du Brinney's rule" which states that no human behavior is engaged in without a psychological reason. So many of us engage in activities which are self-destructive or at least self-damaging. We protest the Church's actions or failures to act; we protest our country's actions or failures to act; we are willing to an alarming degree to accept personal responsibility for poverty, illness, injustice, and human sufferings of every kind. I do not mean to suggest that we have no altruistic reasons for these attitudes and behaviors, or that the theological motivations for these things are untrue. Certainly our mission is to imitate Christ who "became sin" for us, to take on our own shoulders the burden of righting the world's wrongs.

But I do suggest that du Brinney's rule is alive and well: in addition to altruistic motivation and theological explanation there are other forces at work. We are confounded by the Problem of Evil, and we are enraged at God's permitting these injustices to happen. We cannot act aggressively toward God, and so we direct our rage at ourselves and at the institutions that nurture us. We become depressed, and we act in a depressed way. We demonstrate every form of aggression against the self, from the "somatizing" that causes us to stay in bed rather than face the day's insoluble problems to the irrational act of suicide which is the ultimate self-aggression.

Lucy Fuchs, a teacher of sociology and a practicing social worker especially familiar with the interpersonal problems within religious communities, has described some of these symptoms for us.

> Even when every reason to be angry is present and they are simply smoldering, many persons will deny their anger. They will use such expressions as "I am disappointed," "You make me

sad," "I'm not mad at you, just upset." The truth is that they are angry, and the sooner they recognize it the better.

Anger has to come out in one way or another. When it is denied it is likely to show itself in a hundred different undesirable ways. It may take its toll physically. Many illnesses such as headaches, gastro-intestinal or respiratory disorders, skin problems, arthritis, and circulatory problems can be a result, direct or indirect, of anger that is smoldering within.

Anger also takes its toll on community life. An angry sister can be irritable, forever chipping away at the sisters with whom she lives. She can get unduly angry at her students or other charges since this "just anger" is the one acceptable outlet she recognizes. She is in fact not so very angry at her students; she is merely venting all her rage on them.[8]

Healing our anger

If anger at God is a real problem, then it is clear that we must deal with it. Perhaps the first and most important thing we can do is to acknowledge its existence. To continue to be controlled by the taboo against anger at God, to allow that anger to lurk in the dark as an unknown and unknowable reality, is to increase its power. How great is that anger, really? What damage is it capable of doing? Is it truly sinful? If we make it impossible to explore these questions and to begin to answer them, then we will never understand our anger, and we will never have the opportunity to deal with it.

Our goal ought to be "healing anger." On the one hand, we must heal ourselves of our anger at God; we must begin to heal the emotional and spiritual wounds that this anger inflicts on us. On the other hand, accomplishing this kind of healing implies coming to see our anger at God as a healing power in itself.

First, we ought to be able to acknowledge the fact that deep and hidden anger against God is a sign, perhaps the most powerful one, of real faith. We live in an age that struggles with faith; when men and women are filled with doubt. Consciously and unconsciously we do and say many things in an effort to convince others and ourselves that we really do believe in God. If, in the deepest and most spontaneous core of our being we harbor anger at God of the kind I have been describing, then that emotion is a most powerful demonstration that we must believe in him. Many people fear the unknown, but no one can fear what he or she firmly believes does not exist.

Second, we must be able to compare our feelings of rage with those of other people. If there are ways in which our hearts are troubled by our own helplessness, if there are ways in which we resent the power of God that reminds us we are not all-powerful, then we ought to understand that we share those feelings and experiences with our brothers and sisters.

The destructive power of our anger at God lies not in its existence, but in its hiddenness. So long as we repress and deny these feelings of anger they will be redirected toward ourselves, and we will be giving them freedom to destroy us. We can begin to take practical steps towards dealing with the most distasteful things in our personal lives and ministries if only we will rob our anger of its power to attack and consume us.

Endnotes

1. Harold S. Kushner, *When Bad Things Happen to Good People* (New York: Schocken Books, 1981).

2. Leo Madow, M.D., *Anger: How to Recognize and Cope With It* (New York: Charles Scribner's Sons, 1978).

3. Ana-Maria Rizzuto, M.D., *The Birth of the Living God: A Psychoanalytic Study* (Chicago: University of Chicago Press, 1979).

4. Rev. Herbert F. Smith, S.J., "Discovering God's Absence," *Sisters Today* 48:3 (November 1976): 172–182.

5. Karl Stern, *The Third Revolution* (Garden City, NY: Image Books, 1961).

6. See Pierre Wolff, *May I Hate God?* (New York: Paulist Press, 1979).

7. Thomas J. McDonnell, "The Jealousy of God," *Sisters Today* 44:5 (January 1973): 289–297.

8. Lucy Fuchs, "Angry Nuns," *Sisters Today* 46:5 (January 1975): 286–290.

Anger: Destructive and life-giving energy

John A. Struzzo

Self-acceptance • Self-awareness • Self-experience •
Self-expression • The body electric • The inner calm •
Guidelines for transforming anger

Reverend John A. Struzzo, C.S.C., Ph.D., is a full-time psychotherapist at the House of Affirmation in Montara, California. A priest of the Congregation of Holy Cross, Father Struzzo received his bachelor's and master's degrees in theology and sociology at the University of Notre Dame and his doctorate in sociology from Florida State University. For several years Father Struzzo was Professor of Sociology at Northern Illinois University. He then completed a postgraduate certificate in marriage and family psychotherapy at the Institute of Religion and Health in New York City, and interned in clinical psychology at Worcester State Hospital. Before joining the staff of the House of Affirmation, Father Struzzo was executive director of a pastoral counseling center in South Bend, Indiana. He has lectured widely on issues relating to psychology and religion, and on personal growth and development. He is a member of the American Association of Pastoral Counselors, the American Association of Marriage and Family Therapists, and the California Association of Marriage and Family Therapy.

Once there was a Swami who was master of a temple in Bengal. On the path to the temple there lived a cobra that used to bite people on their way to worship. As the incidents increased, everyone became fearful, and many stopped going to the temple. Therefore, Swami told the snake that it was wrong to bite people, and made it promise that it would never do it again. Soon afterwards, a passerby saw the same snake, but it made no attempt to bite him. Soon word spread that the snake had become passive, and the people were no longer afraid of it. It was not long before the village boys, laughing, were dragging the poor snake behind them. Swami returned and summoned the snake to see if it had kept its promise. The cobra miserably approached Swami, who noticed that it was bleeding. Swami said, "Tell me how this happened." The snake was near tears, and cried out that it had been abused ever since it had made the promise. "I told you not to bite," said the Swami, "but I did not tell you not to hiss."[1]

Many of us confuse the hiss with the bite. To control our anger completely and to repress it is to deaden ourselves.

However, the constant direct expression of our anger can lead to the destruction of self and others. Today much emphasis is placed on a catharsis model whereby we are encouraged to discharge our anger. We can do this by talking it out, shouting, exercising, watching violent movies, throwing pillows, or just "letting it all hang out." Repression, we are told, leads to bottled-up anger, resulting in anxiety, depression, alcoholism, sexual problems, and a wide range of psychosomatic symptoms such as high blood pressure and ulcers.

I would argue that neither repression nor the direct expression of anger ultimately resolves anything. The resolution of anger lies in a transformation of its energy into compassion and love. Anger is not our enemy; it is compassion in seed.[2] Ultimately, the issue is how can we transmute all our emotions into an intense feeling for God?

So often I hear clients ask, "How do I get rid of my anger?" Christ answered that question in the parable of the wheat and the weeds. At its conclusion he said, "If you pull up the weeds now, you will pull up the wheat with them. Let them both grow together until the harvest."[3] If we get rid of our anger, we also get rid of our passion—our very life force.

Everything in creation exists in duality, in polar opposites: love and hatred, pleasure and pain, light and darkness. Anger and compassion are two sides of the same coin. How then do we transmute anger into compassion, and ultimately into an intense love for God, for others, and for ourselves?

Self-acceptance

We cannot transform any feeling, including anger, without first accepting and owning it. This means we need to allow ourselves to become fully aware of our anger, without censorship, and without interfering self-criticism; we need to accept responsibility for it and acknowledge the feeling as our own.[4] Such an attitude is not possible if we are preoccupied with moral evaluation. To own our anger would mean honestly acknowledging that this is how we are feeling right now. This is how we are expressing our relationships to other people at this moment. If we permit ourselves to experience our anger and accept it, then we will be free to understand its origin and integrate it into our total personalities.[5]

Many of us mask anger with indifference, or deny and repress it, and thereby build a strong wall around ourselves. Once anger arises, it tends to follow a natural course on its own—"it is experienced; it is expressed in some form of bodily behavior, and is discharged."[6] When this process is blocked by denial or repression, the underlying tension remains. We do not get rid of an emotion by refusing to feel or acknowledge it; we simply disown a part of ourselves. We can silence the voice of anger, but we cannot cancel the message it contains, nor the necessity to deal with it.[7] The price we pay is reduced sensitivity to all feelings—a sense of being empty and dead inside.

Self-awareness

The first step toward acceptance of anger is awareness. I find the simplest method to approach feelings is through body awareness. Our body stores the memories of our mind and emotions. Through its tensions and pain, our body is trying to tell us something. We need to learn to listen to it, to understand the lesson it is trying to teach us.

One technique for getting in touch with your feelings is to imagine your body tensions and pain. First, locate in your body a place where you feel tension. Focus all your attention on that place. Then describe the tension in detail. Ask yourself, how deep is the pain? Is it on the surface, or below the skin? What shape does it have? What color is it? Use your imagination and guess a color, even if you do not see one. How large is it? Feel the tension totally. Focus on the tension without analyzing it. Let the tension tell you what it is about. Become aware of any images or memories that arise while you continue to focus. You may find it helpful to breathe into that spot.

Our body can also express repressed anger through psychosomatic symptoms. Some examples are high blood pressure, ulcers, colitis, chronic neck and back pain, chronic fatigue, sleep disturbances, depression, and boredom. Although any of these conditions could express various meanings they can also be signs of anger.

Anger is expressed in many disguised ways. For example, cynicism or sarcasm often mask anger as can malicious gossip, or telling the truth—not the supportive truth, but one linked to skeletons in the closet, underlying fears and hurts. The truth then can become a cover for intense hostility.[8] Talking behind people's backs is another form of disguised anger. Persons who are overprotective, smothering, or playing the martyr role may also be manifesting a hidden anger.

Some men and women who are out of touch with their anger act it out unconsciously. Their behavior may include chronic neglecting to return borrowed items; bumping into people or spilling things on them; arriving late habitually; breaking appointments at the last minute or missing them altogether; giving misinformation or wrong directions; being sexually provocative or seductive and then frustrating; feeling sorry for others; or having automobile accidents. If you recognize any of these behaviors as your own, you might ask if they are expressions of your anger. Usually such subtle sabotages are directed at loved ones.[9]

Sometimes anger is used to cover up other feelings. Underneath anger is often hurt, fear, helplessness, shame, guilt, or anxiety.[10]

If you experience any of the above symptoms, or if you are feeling annoyed, frustrated, disappointed, hurt, anxious, or in general very tense, ask yourself if you might be angry.[11]

Self-experience

Once we can identify and acknowledge our anger, the next step is to allow ourselves to experience it, to feel it. Experience is different from naming it. Acknowledgement is primarily a cognitive art whereby we say, "Yes, I know that I am angry." Experience is on the level of feeling. What usually prevents an experience of anger is fear, fear of the dark and unknown.[12] A child represses anger (experienced as intolerable) not only because anger is a disvalue, but also because it threatens a sense of control. It causes the child to feel impotent. In later years, the block against reconfronting anger serves the same unconscious purpose—to maintain equilibrium, to protect his or her sense of control and self-esteem. As a child, repression and denial can serve as a means of effective coping and survival. As an adult, those same means often become self-defeating and lower one's self-esteem.[13]

If we could allow ourselves to feel fully our anger, it would be transformed and we would master it. However, to transform our anger we must take it inside and learn to sit with it and befriend it, rather than discharge it outwardly. Nevertheless external expression is often an intermediate step toward transformation, especially for those who have repressed their anger.[14]

There is a story told of a spiritual master who had two disciples. The first disciple crossed the river in a boat. While aboard he overheard his companions criticizing his master, calling him a fraud and a hypocrite. The disciple became furious and threateneed to sink the boat. When the disciple later reported to his master what had happened, his master rebuked him and taught him to resist and turn the other cheek. On another occasion, the second disciple was crossing the same river. Again his fellow travellers were criticizing his master and spreading false rumors about him. Although distressed, the disciple remained silent feeling there was nothing he could do about it. Besides, he thought, they do not know what they are talking about. When he reported the incident to his master, the master reproved him for allowing such slander in his presence.

The first disciple already knew how to resist people and needed to learn nonviolence. The second disciple acted out of cowardice, and needed to learn to be more assertive.[15]

When and how to deal with our anger is a developmental issue. For someone who has long repressed feelings, it is often necessary to express outwardly the anger as a step toward its integration and transformation into compassion. For someone who is already able to experience and express anger, the next step is to learn how to transmute this energy into compassion and love, and a deep feeling for God.

Self-expression

Is outwardly expressing our anger helpful? If we express our anger, generally we will feel some temporary relief, since suspended energy is burdensome and heavy. The principle that it is better to express than suppress is generally true. However, direct expression can also be destructive of self and others. Also, expression can sometimes have the opposite effect intended; instead of releasing anger, it can inflame it.[16]

Seymour Feshbach concluded from experiments with children that when they are permitted to play aggressively, they do not become less aggressive as a catharsis model would predict, but rather more aggressive. Similarly, Leonard Berkowitz found that shouting as a means of ventilation of anger had no effect on the reduction of anger. Murray Strauss argues that there is an element of truth in catharsis, but not in the usual sense of physiological relief. If a person does not deal with the underlying cause of anger, it will remain or even worsen.[17] Carol Tavris, in reviewing the literature on catharsis, concludes that the catharsis model does not really work. She argues that talking out your anger does not reduce it, but rehearses it. As you recite your grievances, your emotional arousal builds up, making you feel as angry as you did when the infuriating event first happened. At the same time Tavris concedes that discussing one's anger can lead to greater clarity and practical solutions.[18]

Ultimately, the decision as to whether or not to express our anger rests on what we hope to communicate and what goal we want to achieve. However, these two concerns can be in conflict.[19] What may be an appropriate response of anger toward our spouse or lover may be inappropriate toward our boss. Sometimes emotional release feels good, not because we have emptied some physiological reservoir, but because we have accomplished some social goal like the redemption of justice, or the reinforcement of social order. In working through our anger, it is important to redefine the situation, and not just lower our pulse rate, since anger involves both mind and body.

How we perceive a situation determines our emotional response to it. To feel a sense of release in a cathartic way demands that we know what we are angry about and what the outside circumstances are. How we feel will also depend on the other person's response—especially if we feel heard and understood. If our listener remains silent or is defensive, the chances are we will become even angrier. Thus, ventilating anger can be cathartic, but only if it restores our sense of control and reduces our belief that we are helpless or powerless.[20]

We need to distinguish acknowledging and experiencing our anger from acting it out. We can learn to be more assertive, and say what we really feel, instead of resentfully bearing grudges. We can learn to talk about our anger in such a way that we do not insult others or escalate the disagreement. We can talk about our feelings and describe our emotional reactions without attacking others.[21]

The weight of evidence suggests that acting out anger generally makes us angrier, and simply solidifies an existing hostile attitude. If we could keep quiet about momentary irritations, and distract ourselves until our fury dies down, the chances are we will feel better. This is not to suggest that we should harbor resentments, or sulk in silence.[22] In the heat of the moment our perception is distorted and we often say things which leave scars and can later return to haunt us. In our attempt to hurt others by our anger, we end up hurting ourselves.

To understand this process we need to review what Einstein has taught us: all matter is energy and all energy is convertible into matter. God's creative energy is manifest in all reality, in rocks, plants, animals, sexuality, anger, and the soul. What differentiates reality is different degrees of vibrations and consciousness. All energy is therefore one.[23]

The body electric

Our bodies are electromagnetic energy fields. Every time we pass a current through an electric wire, we create a magnetic field. Our nervous system transmits scientifically measurable electrical impulses, and in so doing sets up its own magnetic field.

The essential feature of magnetism is its power of attraction and repulsion. Divine love is magnetic; so also are human love, happiness, hatred, fear, and anger—every state of consciousness which is actively manifest. Thus love attracts love, fear attracts its object, and negativity begets negativity. If our energy flow is directed toward a particular person, and if there exists on any level in that individual a similar state of awareness (and therefore magnetism), we would repel or attract the person, depending on whether the interchange is sympathetic or antipathetic. Thus while hatred and anger are negative, and might seem to exert only a repelling force, they become attractive if they are reciprocated in another person. Love, on the other hand, although apparently purely attractive in its influence, if not reciprocated can become a repulsive force causing mutual separation.

When we send out a strong thought with its corresponding feeling, a ray of energy goes out from us toward the object of our thought. This energy ray creates its own magnetic field—strong or weak according to the relative strength of our will. Thus when we are angry toward someone, we not only send negative energy toward him or her, but also attract negativity to ourselves. This is why when we feel angry everything seems to go wrong. Thus it is possible by negative thoughts to harm others and similarly, in turn, to harm ourselves. To think negatively about others ultimately results in greater harm to ourselves. Similarly, to bless others attracts to ourselves the greatest blessings.[24]

Not only do negative attitudes, feelings, and behaviors cause potential harm to others, they disrupt the balance of the universe: when our energy runs contrary to the evolutionary life force it is negatively polarized. Our collective negativity can create meteorological and geological imbalances which lead to storms, floods, hurricanes, and upheavals such as volcanoes and earthquakes. Ultimately wars are the results of our negative thought forms. If a nation strongly fears war, it will attract to itself the object of its fears. The massive consciousness focused on defense and fear in this country attracts to itself what it seeks to avoid. Likewise, if we learn to live in harmony with the natural laws of the universe, and live by hope and love rather than by fears and negativity, we can reduce the severity of cosmological disturbances.

Physical effects are generated by physical means. However, their root source is in the consciousness of individuals and groups. Physical effects always have their source in spiritual causes. Once we realize this, we can control and change our destiny, by changing our consciousness and by becoming attuned to the divine rhythms of the universe. As we sow, so shall we reap (Galatians 6:7).

Thus each person is a channel through which the infinite energy of the universe flows, and which is transformed by the individual's consciousness. We create our subjective worlds as the result of the energy we transmit and create.[25]

The outward expression of anger is often a necessary and helpful stage toward self-awareness and ownership of our feelings. Ultimately our goal is to neutralize our emotions so that we can transmute our feelings into an intense feeling for God. It is helpful here to distinguish feelings from emotions. Feelings are our inner experience of energy. Emotions are our reactive process. Thus emotions are an outward expression of feeling. When we express emotions we deplete and lower our energy. If we express them inwardly we intensify our energy and transmute it.[26] Thus our goal is to control our energy, intensify it, and direct it upward to God. God vibrates at a very high level of intensity. Therefore, to spiritualize anger and feelings in general means learning to conserve energy.

The inner calm

Negative emotions such as fear, anger, and guilt pull our energy downward. But if we take this energy and learn to sit with it in a positive, accepting way, it becomes intensified and transformed. However, before we can learn to express anger inwardly, we need first to be in possession of it, and assume responsibility for it. We can not overcome negative emotions by simply pushing the pendulum in the opposite direction. We need to enter into the depths of our inner center and look at the outside world from that place of calm and neutrality. This process does not make us stoical or unfeeling. Rather we master our feelings. We do not have to react to external provocations, but can learn to act out of our own inner center.[27]

Any time we react under intense emotions, we distort reality. It is like seeing our reflection in a pool. If the waters are disturbed, our image will be cloudy and distorted. If the water is calm, then we will be able to see a clear picture of ourselves. It is helpful, therefore, first to pull back from strong emotions and look at the situation from a detached place. This behavior is different from suppression, which is running from the emotion. We need to acknowledge our feelings, and not deny them. Often when we act under the influence of strong emotions, we say or do something we will later regret. Thus if we are angry, we should pull back and look at the anger dispassionately. A technique to help us become detached is to project on a screen the provocative situation that triggered our anger. As we watch the event, we should breathe deeply several times. This process will help to neutralize the event for us.[28] Emotions, including anger, are neither bad nor good. What we do with them is a moral matter. Conditions outside of us are basically neutral. We cannot make the world perfect, but we can change ourselves, and in turn the world will be changed.[29]

If we can learn to remain at rest in our center, we will not be affected by outside frustrations and provocations. The core of our inner reality is our soul, where God is realized. That core remains unchanged. When we enter into that core, the world around us moves, but we remain calm. Then when we do react, it will be from that center. From there we can express feeling, empathize, but we do not react in a personal way. Then our energy is intensified and we feel continual joy. If we react outwardly we feel emptied and drained. If we do not know our center we will lead a life that is rootless, meaningless, empty.[30]

When we are capable of reuniting our energy with our inner center, its original source, we have mastered our emotions. Energy is neither love nor hate nor anger, but simply energy. The same energy becomes anger, becomes love, becomes hate, becomes sexual. These emotions are all forms of the same energy. We create the form, and energy moves into it. If we love deeply, we will not have much energy to be angry. When energy goes back to its original source, it becomes formless, pure energy. Thus the ultimate resolution to the question, "What do I do with my anger?" is to do nothing. If we go back to its inner source, we will feel powerful and become magnetized.[31]

Guidelines for transforming anger

Taking responsibility

How can we transform anger into compassion and love? First, we need to realize that basically we create our own responses; we are not the victims of outside circumstances. Of course we do not usually feel this way, and we will need a lot of spiritual growth to move toward this awareness. Others are a mirror of ourselves. According to Jung, we project outwardly both the positive and negative aspects of our personality, which we have not yet acknowledged or assimilated. When we come into contact with those parts, they appear to be outside of ourselves. Thus, what angers us about others is a part of ourselves mirrored by them. Ultimately, our experience of the world, including our relationships, is the projected experience of our inner being. The outside and inside worlds are in reality one.[32]

As long as we believe that the social and natural environments are the cause of our current situation, we make ourselves helpless and avoid taking responsibility for our lives. To the extent that we are able to acknowledge responsibility for our situation, we are able to take control and change it.[33] Consequently, when we are able to acknowledge that the source of our anger is within us, only then can we transform its energy into compassion and love.

Accepting what is

Next, we need to learn to accept what is. Often our anger is rooted in our sense of powerlessness, whereby we want to change what is basically unchangeable. If we perceive the source of anger outside ourselves, we feel powerless and thereby only intensify its energy. Frequently, in attempting to talk out differences, we get into power struggles. We try to change others, and convince them of what we perceive as the truth. We experience ourselves as right and the others as wrong. When compromise or change seems impossible, the real solution is to change our consciousness and accept what is. Let others have their opinions, prejudices, and even what may appear as obvious errors. If we change our expectations then there will be no problem. Anger is often the result of the frustration of some personal desire or goal. If we let go of the expectation and accept what is, then we are redefining the situation and the source of our anger will dissipate.

This flexibility does not mean we will not continue to work for change, or fight for justice and truth. The issue is one of consciousness. Our conscious mind perceives the world in terms of duality: either-or, good or bad, right or wrong. With this consciousness we are constantly reacting and experiencing ups and downs. When we see the world in unity rather than in duality, then we realize we are all alike and we learn to tune in to the heart and center of others. We are able then to see the world through the eyes of others and realize from their point of view that they are right, even as we are right from our point of view. Then instead of reacting out of our likes and dislikes, we act out of our own center according to what is the most useful response.

Sometimes the most useful response might be to display anger as Christ did when he drove the money changers from the temple. This anger is rooted in compassion and love. If we are playing baseball, and the pitcher is throwing fast balls, we do not say, "I wish he wouldn't do that," and get angry; we adjust our hitting stance to the one that will be most effective. Likewise, when we are centered and neutral, our responses will be helpful and compassionate.

Thus when we feel intense emotion, we should wait until we calm down, until we are centered and grounded, before we act. Then we will be better able to see situations and people as they are, rather than as we wish them to be. Whatever comes our way, we must take it within, and there find the response that will be the most loving, constructive, and useful.[34]

Useful responses to anger from others

When others are angry at us, what is the most useful response? In general, we can choose one of three stances: resistance, affinity, or nonresistance. In resisting the anger, our body becomes tense and we put up a wall, or actively fight back. However, we become what we resist. Resistance will only increase our anger, and disturb our inner peace.

We are in affinity when we allow ourselves to feel the anger of the other—to be empathic. The problem here is that there may be confusion over the ownership of the feeling. True compassion exists when we feel empathy for the other, but also when we remain in control of our own boundaries and energy. We have confidence in others' ability to solve their problems and work through their feelings.

Sometimes it is difficult to experience compassion. In that case the most useful response may be nonresistance. When we are in nonresistance, we are neutral to the energy coming toward us. We watch it pass through us to the other side without judging it.[35] To facilitate nonresistance we can imagine our body is glass and the anger a red light that passes right through it.

Forgiveness

The more we are able to respond to anger in others in a calm, compassionate way out of our innermost core, the more we will be forgiving. Forgiveness is not so much an action as an inner transformation of our heart. To forgive means to let go—to release. Usually when we hold a grudge or feel resentment against others we expect them to apologize first, or in some way to make up for the hurt they have caused us. True forgiveness is unconditional love.

An aid toward forgiveness is to pray for those at whom we are angry. At first such prayer will feel hypocritical. But since our thoughts affect our feelings, in time sincere loving and forgiving thoughts will release our anger, and transform it into love and compassion.[36]

When we respond with love, we create a shield that protects us from the negative energy of others. If hostile thoughts are aimed at us, they will rebound and be flung back toward the sender. Thus a pure heart and mind are protectors against inimical assaults, and the sender suffers the destructive effects he or she had intended to cause us.[37]

Solitude

As Henri Nouwen well puts it, "solitude is the furnace of transformation." It is in solitude that we come face to face with our inner world and true self. It is in solitude that anger and greed show their faces. There we give long hostile speeches to our enemies, and entertain all kinds of destructive fantasies. It is there that we encounter the demons that feed our illusions. But it is also in solitude that we encounter the Lord,[38] and in that encounter we discover our true self.

There we learn that we are not this body and these emotions. Rather we are spiritual persons manifest in material form. Our task is not to become holy but to realize that we are already holy, united with God and all creation. God is already within us. Our goal is not to become different, but to recognize and experience who we really are and to live out that reality. We have everything we need right now to be perfect.

Meditation

One of the most important means of this self-realization is regular, deep meditation. Through meditation our mind, nervous system, emotions, and physical body are harmonized and transformed.

Meditation is a one-pointed concentration of our energy on God. Light from the sun is powerful. However, if we take that same light and focus it through a magnifying glass or laser, it becomes even more powerful. Likewise if we can focus all our energy at one point, we have the power to move mountains.

Through meditation we attune ourselves to the living Spirit within. As we pursue the practice of meditation, we open our storehouse of gifts and talents. Stumbling blocks become stepping stones. Obstacles become opportunities. The more we attune ourselves to the Spirit within, the more we come to know ourselves.

Scriptures tell us, "Be still and know that I am God" (Ps. 46:10). Meditation requires stillness of mind and body. One of the most helpful practices in quieting the mind and body is deep breathing. Alternate nostril breathing in particular helps to balance our energies, and thereby neutralize our emotions. The use of a mantra can also help to purify our mind and emotions. "Blessed are the pure of heart for they shall see God" (Matt 5:8).

One of the main reasons for knowing ourselves is to become greater channels for the expression of the living Spirit in our service of and love for others. By changing ourselves we help to change groups, organizations, governments, and nations.

Such a task seems overwhelming. Christ reminds us that we are like yeast which leavens the whole loaf of bread. Thus, Abraham was told if he could find ten righteous people, Sodom and Gomorrah would not be destroyed. So, if only one person lives in attunement with the life-giving Spirit, he or she could change the lives of ten others, and if those ten so live, they could change the lives of one hundred persons, and so on. If we keep multiplying by the tenth power we will eventually reach the population of the world.

Through regular and deep meditation, we experience the Kingdom of God within. We become identified with the object of our deep concentration. The more we look inward at our true self, the closer we are to discovering our true destiny. The more we attune ourselves to the God within and without, the more we will be able to spiritualize our emotions and transform anger into compassion and love.[39]

Conclusion

Life is basically an outward manifestation of our consciousness through the medium of the energy that we generate. Even the undesired and unexpected is drawn to us because of some attitude in our mind. A man or woman who repeatedly thinks and acts like a criminal will become a criminal. If the person began thinking and acting like a saint with as much force, he or she would become one.[40] The same energy used to animate an old habit can be used to animate a new one. Thus one who experiences deep, intense anger has the potentiality for deep and intense compassion.

If we continue to think of ourselves as angry and unforgiving, we simply reinforce that consciousness. If we begin to think of ourselves as forgiving and loving, our anger will be transformed. However, it is impossible to be forgiving and loving of others without also being forgiving and loving of ourselves.

When we continue to express anger outwardly we reinforce our hostile attitude. If we learn to take our anger inside and offer it up to the Lord, it will be transformed into compassion and love. The first step toward compassion is accepting ourselves as we are right now.

Like every ideal, this one is a lifetime goal. Compassion must begin with self-understanding and self-love in the present moment; we need patience with ourselves. As long as we orient ourselves toward the goal of transforming our emotions, we will reach it, since it is God's work in us and with us. As Paul preached to the Philippians, "I am quite cèrtain that the One who began this good work in you will see that it is finished when the Day of Christ Jesus comes" (1:6–7).[41]

Endnotes

1. Carol Tavris, *Anger: The Misunderstood Emotion* (New York: Simon and Schuster, 1982), p. 26.
2. Bhagwan Shree Rajneesh, *The Book of the Secrets* (San Francisco: Harper Colophon Books, 1977), p. 34.
3. J.B. Phillips, trans. *The New Testament in Modern English* (New York: Macmillan, 1962), pp. 41–42.
4. Nathaniel Branden, *The Disowned Self* (New York: Bantam Books, 1974), pp. 89–90.
5. Ibid., p. 91.
6. Ibid., p. 27.
7. Ibid., pp. 27–28.
8. Theodore Rubin, *The Angry Book* (New York: Collier Books, 1969), pp. 120–139.
9. Ibid., pp. 107–109.
10. Muriel Schiffman, *Self Therapy* (Menlo Park, Cal.: Self Therapy Press, 1967), p. 136.
11. Leo Meadow, *Anger: How to Recognize and Cope With It* (New York: Charles Scribner's Sons, 1972), p. 108.
12. Rajneesh, *The Book of the Secrets,* p. 288.
13. Branden, *The Disowned Self,* p. 72.
14. Swami Ajaya, *Psychotherapy East and West* (Honesdale, Pa.: The Himalayan International Institute of Yoga Science and Philosophy of the U.S.A., 1983), p. 266.
15. Swami Probhavananda, *The Sermon on the Mount According to Vedanta* (New York: Mentor Books, 1972), pp. 64–65.
16. Tavris, *Anger: The Misunderstood Emotion,* p. 127.
17. Ibid., pp. 128–129.
18. Ibid., pp. 132–135.
19. Ibid., p. 123.
20. Ibid., pp. 144–149.
21. Ibid., p. 149.
22. Ibid., p. 144.
23. Michael Talbot, *Mysticism and the New Physics* (New York: Bantam Books, 1980), p. 143.
24. Shirley G. Luthman, *Energy and Personal Power* (San Rafael, Cal.: Mehetabel, 1982), pp. 56–69.
25. Jeffrey Goodman, *We Are the Earthquake Generation* (New York: Berkeley Books, 1982), pp. 187–194.
26. Moira Timms, *Prophecies, Predictions* (Santa Cruz, Cal.: Orenda/Unity Press, 1980).

27. Swami Kriyanada, "How to Work With Your Emotions," (Nevada City, Cal.: Ananda Recordings, 1984), taped lecture.
28. Ibid.
29. Roy Eugene Davis, *Studies In Truth* (Lakemont, Ga.: C.S.A. Press, 1981), p. 110.
30. Kriyanada, "How to Work With Your Emotions."
31. Rajneesh, *The Book of the Secrets,* p. 211.
32. Ibid., pp. 386-390.
33. Ajaya, *Psychotherapy: East and West,* pp. 62, 66.
34. Kriyanada, "How to Work With Your Emotions."
35. Petey Stevens, *Opening Up To Your Psychic Self* (Berkeley, Cal.: Nevertheless Press, 1983), pp. 239-240, 255-256.
36. Gerald G. Jampolsky, M.D., *Teach Only Love* (New York: Bantam Books, 1983), pp. 109-117.
37. Annie Besant and Charles W. Leadbeater, "Thought-Forms," in *The Human Aura,* ed. by Nicholas Regush (New York: Berkeley Books, 1981), pp. 113-122.
38. Henri J.M. Nouwen, *The Way of The Heart* (New York: Ballantine Books, 1983), p. 13.
39. Herbert B. Puryear, *The Edgar Cayce Primer* (New York: Bantam Books, 1982), pp. 234-237.
40. Kriyanada, "How to Work With Your Emotions."
41. Swami Kriyanada, *14 Steps to Perfect Joy* (Nevada City, Cal.: Ananda Publications, 1971), Step 7, pp. 2-3.

Anger on behalf of justice

Miriam D. Ukeritis

What is this anger? • Adolescent anger • Levels of anger •
Passionate anger • Passion in the quest for justice •
Resistance to anger on behalf of justice • When is it a sin not to
be angry?

Miriam D. Ukeritis, C.S.J., Ph.D., is a full-time psychotherapist at the House of Affirmation in Hopedale, Massachusetts. She pursued her graduate education and received a doctorate in clinical psychology from the University of Pittsburgh. For several years, Sister Ukeritis served as director of the Counseling for Laity program of the Diocese of Albany, New York. She has taught at the college level, given numerous workshops and lectures, and is a member of many professional associations, including the American Psychological Association.

When I was asked if I would present a paper at this symposium, we, as a staff and residential community, were in the middle of a week-long seminar on women. "Feelings" were rampant that week as women reflected on their experiences, and men reacted to the process. Many experienced frustration at the lack of a "definition" of woman. Personally, I was aware of my own frustration, as a psychologist, with the task of calling women to grow in their self-esteem in the midst of a social structure that screams they (we) are second class. As a vowed religious, I was also acutely aware of the tension I know in being part of an ecclesiastical structure that by its public policy and subtle seduction denies the reality that women are also created in the image of God.

So, I decided I might have something to say on the topic of anger. Knowing how powerful a force it has been and continues to be for my own growth, I wanted to share some of the stages I have experienced in the process of befriending this emotion. I would also like to indicate where it has taken me and many others on the road of Christian discipleship.

While I will not focus exclusively on the topic of women and the Church, many examples will come from that experience. It is only one area, though, where anger and justice meet. My hope is to present a broader perspective.

You may have noted a familiar ring to the title of this presentation. It comes from the 1971 Synod of Bishops, which reminded us that "action on behalf of justice and participation in the transformation of the world fully appears to us as a constitutive dimension of the preaching of the Gospel." Reverend J. Bryan Hehir, a noted advocate of social justice, remarked that if a man approaching orders were to state that he really did not care to be involved in sacramental ministry, there would be no question about his being denied orders. However, if such an individual were to state that he was not "called" to ministry in the area of social justice, such a drastic response would, sadly enough, probably not be forthcoming. In light of the above statement, must not our response be other?

The desire to work for social justice is often precipitated by an experience of anger. Hence we can look at anger in the context of the mandate to work for justice. I would like to explore the reasons why we resist this experience of anger, as well as the notion that *not* being angry may itself be sinful (in contrast to the old teaching that anger is a sin).

What is this anger?

I would like to begin by recalling a conversation I had with a friend. We were enjoying some "catching up" over a cup of coffee when she remarked that, on her drive to my house, she had passed two vans of college students with placards supporting the Nestlé boycott. I smiled and commented that it, indeed, was a day for frisbees and causes. She was rather chagrined by my response, particularly because of the many times we had worked together on justice issues. I saw, however, a clear connection between the two.

Adolescent anger

Perhaps because I am aware of my own affiliation with "causes" as a part of my adolescent experience, and also because of my work with individuals in a variety of justice projects, I am aware that groups fighting for "causes" are wonderful for individuals who need to be angry as a part of their developmental task. This is not the anger on behalf of justice of which I write. It is, however, an expression of anger that frequently sours persons on the issue of justice, and results in their affiliation with the opposite cause. How often have you experienced people whose militance was so aggressive that you wanted to do the opposite of what they were advocating simply because they were advocating it? That reaction is somewhat akin to rejecting the Church because some members are less than exemplary.

There is, however, a value to this "immature anger." (And remember, immature is not synonymous with bad. There are clearly times in one's life when it is appropriate to be immature!) Such anger gives the individual something outside self to rebel against. Adolescents, in defining themselves as against this evil, are faithful to the adolescent process of self-definition in external rather than internal terms. By opposing the nuclear arms race the adolescent is identifying with others who are also against this evil. Again, we see another adolescent dynamic: self-definition by membership in a group. It is out of that context that the adolescent can find a space with others of that group to discover what it is that he or she is for, thereby moving toward an establishment of identity and inner authority.

Clearly, this stage is often resolved through a loss of idealism, further anger that the cause itself is not perfect, or the movement toward commitments that are closer to the newly-formed identity. In speaking of this experience in terms of disenchantment, William Bridges makes a clear distinction between the disenchanted person who recognizes the old view as sufficient in its time but insufficient now, and the disillusioned person, who rejects the embodiment of this view.[1] The disenchanted person moves on, but the disillusioned person stops and goes through the play again with new actors.[2]

Levels of anger

There are other aspects of anger that frequently masquerade as anger on behalf of justice, but which are, rather, levels of expression.

The first level is that of selfishness or "do it my way!" It comes out of an attitude akin to "if I'm doing it, everybody should!" That means that if I am "into" the charismatic renewal, you have to find Jesus the way I have found him. If I am involved in pro-life politics no one who is outside of my single issue campaign is interested in life. Feminists coming from such a stance tell us that we cannot know our oppression as women until we totally reject all men.

There is a fundamental self-righteousness about such a belief system. It is based on a black and white mentality that is neither tolerant of the differences with which we are marked nor appreciative of God's gift of freedom. It is a very primitive level of anger, and does not revere the other person. And God help you if you are an object of my campaign for justice: you had better want what I am working for you to have!

A second level of this anger is self-serving: "I'll be hurt if you don't work with me. The consequences will be disastrous to me." My expression of that level came to me the other night as I was driving home and encountered the third vehicle of the evening without headlights on. As I frantically flashed my lights and honked my horn, I muttered, "Jerk, put your lights on!" Sensitive as I am to the issue of anger, I reflected on its source and named it as the concern about my own safety. "I am angry with you because you are a threat to my life." Or "This thing is threatening my life and, therefore, you should be concerned about it."

Such attitudes are found in the anger of the anti-nuclear activists whose concern is based solely on the fact that radiation from the nearby plant is harmful to their health or is devaluing the real estate. Its focus stays within the individual's narrow sphere of interest. There is usually a gap or chasm between "my concern" about that issue and justice issues not directly related to "my" self-interest.

Let us not be naive, however. Clearly, there are times when this anger is appropriate. Last week, for example, the mechanic "fixed" my car so that it had more problems when I drove out of the garage than when I drove in. I was angry—for me! Such anger is sometimes what keeps us alive.

The third level of anger is altruistic: "Let's be faithful to celebrating life!" It is akin to the anger of God that comes from a deep convenantal relationship based on the promise of life; God's concern extends beyond the confines of my family, friends, interests, and favorite causes. Though I do not have a personal (experiential) connection with other groups and/or individuals, their ability to live life to the fullest, as was promised by Jesus, is a prime concern to me.

A true experience of anger involves the total person—intellect, emotions, spirit. It is the anger of the prophet who, frequently in spite of her or himself, is compelled to speak the truth as it is experienced.

This experience of the truth is a critical part of anger. It involves a vulnerability that takes me beyond myself and my narrow circles and puts me in touch with the totality of creation. "Save the whales" takes on meaning deeper than the anger at unfeeling, profiteering whaling fleets. The exclusion of women from aspects of ministry is felt as the robbing of the entire community of the giftedness of that individual and the particular word of God that would be spoken only through her. The unbridled clericalism in our Church is experienced as rape—the imposition of another's thoughts, needs, and styles on others who have no access to the power structure and whose needs, inclinations, and indeed humanness are ignored. It was out of such an experience of anger that Jesus cleansed the temple and excoriated the Pharisees who tithed mint and other herbs, and ignored the weightier matters of the Covenant.

Passionate anger

An example of passionate anger can be found in Matthew's Gospel account of the king who held a banquet and found that the invited guests did not plan to attend. The experience of inviting others to the fullness of life, and having them delay or reject the invitation gave rise to real anger on the part of the king.

Such anger does not come easily. It presupposes a deep understanding of life and the riches that are offered, as well as a love for all humanity. It arises from knowledge of the breadth of the invitation, and the assurance that there is enough for everyone's need, as Gandhi observed, but not for everyone's greed. Probably, this anger can be experienced only by one who is all merciful. I expect, however, that all of us experience anger on each of the levels I have described.

Michael Crosby speaks of passionate anger in his *Spirituality of the Beatitudes*[3] After making a distinction between the spirit of anger and the emotion of anger (something spontaneous, beyond our control), he points out that in the context of our Scriptures, anger is justified when it reflects a break in promised covenantal relationships: the guests who agreed to partake of the banquet do not appear. The Hebrew Scriptures record this for us in chapter 54 of Isaiah.

> For a brief moment I abandoned you,
> but with great tenderness I will take you back.
> In an outburst of wrath, for a moment
> I hid my face from you;

But with enduring love I take pity on you,
says the Lord, your redeemer.
This is for me like the days of Noah,
when I swore that the waters of Noah
should never again deluge the earth;
So I have sworn not to be angry with you, or to rebuke you.
Though the mountains leave their place
and the hills be shaken,
My love shall never leave you
nor my covenant of peace be shaken,
says the Lord, who has mercy on you
(Is. 54:7–10).

Passion in the quest for justice

The above reading is a passionate statement of God's love for his/her people. It is also a passionate statement of anger. Passion is an element that is often missing in the true quest for justice. In our work on behalf of justice, we cannot afford to be lukewarm or tepid.

Passion on behalf of justice—indeed, on behalf of life—is not a new notion. Yet it is one that we insist on forgetting as we rationalize our response to the invitation to the banquet of life. True, this forgetfulness is reinforced by a spiritual/ascetical tradition that considers passions and feelings inferior and always in need of control. Recall à Kempis who described himself as "weighed down by passions" and counseled us to "fight against your passions," and "get rid of passion and desire."

Matthew Fox, of the creation tradition, presents an alternative approach to passion. Citing the advice of the thirteenth century mystic, Meister Eckhart, to "put on them a bridle of love" instead of repressively controlling passions such as desire and moral outrage (anger), Fox reminds us that a "bridle is a steering device one puts on a presumably energetic horse."[4] He goes on to contrast it to the ascetic tradition which would "control the stallion in each of us by cutting off a leg or by putting a hundred-pound sack of potatoes on its back." Fox is suggesting that we learn to make the passion work for us, to take us and the community into areas where we need to go. We must remember, however, that the bridle itself is a loving bridle, not an instrument of torture—yet, it is very real.

Resistance to anger on behalf of justice

Having had our own sense of altruism touched, we might ask, why talk about resistance? Isn't it obvious that any well-intentioned, intelligent, and enlightened human being (like ourselves) would be delighted to be moved and motivated by such passion? Let us be honest. I did mention the prophets as exemplars of this last style of anger. And what happened to them? They have been rejected, mocked, misunderstood, ostracized, ignored, and even murdered. Not a pleasant fate. And we, by and large, do not want such a destiny for ourselves. So let us look more closely at some of the other sources of resistance.

Powerlessness

If I speak and act on behalf of justice, I have no guarantee that others will listen. In fact, I will probably be overwhelmed and discouraged by my own littleness. Women have been subservient for eons. Why do I think that I can change anything by asking questions? I will just be frustrated and more angry. As I was preparing this essay I wrote to a friend in Nicaragua and asked for her reflections. Many of them are included here. One of her observations was directly related to powerlessness:

> I think that we resist this anger because the issues seem so big and we don't know how to do a structural analysis to do a systemic change. To work for social justice is not like going into a fast food place and coming out with a systemic change. Systemic change is a long, hard, time-consuming, sometimes blood-shedding ordeal. I think anger is resisted because most people do not have time to do this or may not know where to begin.

We like to see results. It takes a lot of discipline, deep maturity—a real dying to self—to work and see little or no result. The egoist, the one who needs to see that "I make a difference," has no place here.

Pain

It hurts to be rejected and misunderstood, not to mention being made fun of! It is also painful to become vulnerable to injustice. As long as I do not know that others are suffering, I do not have to make any response. As long as I think all is rosy in my neighborhood, Church, community, and family, I do not have to deal with the inevitable consequences of being human—that is, being limited, imperfect, and in process.

Knowledge can be painful. When I read that the money required to provide adequate food, water, education, health, and housing for everyone in the world has been estimated at $17 billion a year, about as much as the world spends on arms every two weeks, what else but pain can I experience?

Fear and insecurity

"I'm not quite sure this is something that I should act on. Maybe I'll make a fool of myself." When I stood on the picket line at the grocery store and asked shoppers to buy union lettuce to support the farmworkers, I did not have much of a response to the steelworker who asked me if I belonged to a union. I am all too aware of the inconsistencies in my own life. How dare I speak for justice in situation A when I myself am an oppressor in situation B? Even more, speaking out for justice may truly call me to question seriously my lifestyle. I am not sure if I am ready to surrender so much!

Anger of others

Having someone angry with me is not a pleasant situation. When a family member works for a defense contractor, how can I easily leaflet at the company gate in protest of their policies?

I know that many in my own congregation will insist on the traditional eucharistic celebration at a community event, which involves importing someone who has not participated in the spirit of the day(s) to simply "confect" the eucharist. So, how do I speak on behalf of a liturgical celebration that flows from the hearts of those involved, celebrates the presence of the Spirit of God in the bread and wine of the joys and pains of my sisters, and affirms our women as leaders of prayer and eucharist?

Other consequences of working for justice may include ostracism by a group, particularly loved ones. One can be fired from a job or passed over at the time of promotion. I know of women religious who have been rejected as leaders of their groups because of their clear stance for the poor, for women, and for human liberation.

Inappropriate guilt

Let us not forget the "truth" that we learned long ago: anger is a sin. In acting on behalf of justice, we experience our passion and so, feel guilty. We think: I should not feel that strongly. I should be able to control myself. I should be patient. I should be understanding. I should not upset others. I should turn the other cheek. (Or turn the cheeks of others—victims—to the oppressor, when I see unjust situations in which the voiceless poor or minorities are involved.) All these myths, coming from old tapes that assure us everything will be fine in the next life so endure this one, are simply that—myths! The spirituals of the Black people in our country kept them in slavery; they found solace in religion rather than speak, as they have more recently, for their dignity in this life, in this world, in this time.

Lack of control or guarantees

Many of us who have a clear need to control, experience this fear. If I do allow myself to feel, what will happen? Will I become that unbridled stallion galloping off the edge of a cliff? If something does start in response to my action or the voicing of my opinion, then what? That is when trust in the goodness of God, the leading of the Spirit, and the support of those around me is important. My friend in Nicaragua made a strong statement regarding support:

> Usually when people are working to change unjust structures they hardly ever work alone, so they experience a collective anger and are able to share their anger with others in order not to make it personal. ... It is good not to eat, drink, and sleep it; it is best to find outside interests!

When is it a sin not to be angry?

Anger is powerful, a potentially immensely creative passion. We can compare it to love whose opposite, in terms of energy, is not hate but apathy. If the opposite of anger is non-feeling, numbness, death, then anger might be considered a virtue. Thus, we could define anger as a habit of passionate devotion to all humanity's participation in the banquet of life, and staunch opposition to all that is death-dealing. In this case, anger is a virtue.

Thus, not to be angry can be a sin when I choose to be deaf to the cries of the poor; when I prefer blindness to seeing the pathos of humanity around me; and when I am determined to harden my heart to anything "out there" that may question the comfort and security I experience. If I deliberately choose apathetic to passionate living, I believe that I am failing in the call to choose life, and as long as I am unfaithful to that call to come and celebrate the banquet of life, I sin.

Not to be angry is a sin when my lack of passion condones a death-dealing situation. I cannot witness to complicity with a situation that is anti-life.

Anger on behalf of justice involves the risk of truly living. Let us live passionate lives, celebrating the call to share in the banquet of life, singing with the psalmist the song of justice and mercy and life!

Endnotes

1. William Bridges, *Transitions: Making Sense of Life's Changes* (Reading, Mass.: Addison-Wesley, 1980).

2. Ibid., p. 101.

3. Michael Crosby, O.F.M. Cap., *Spirituality of the Beatitudes* (Maryknoll, N.Y.: Orbis Books, 1980), p. 157.

4. Matthew Fox, *Original Blessing* (Sante Fe, N.M.: Bear and Company, 1983), p. 60.